MAKING TASK GROUPS
WORK IN YOUR WORLD

T0668780

◆

MAKING TASK GROUPS WORK IN YOUR WORLD

Diana Hulse-Killacky
University of New Orleans

Jim Killacky
Tulane University

Jeremiah Donigian
*State University of New York College
at Brockport*

Upper Saddle River, New Jersey
Columbus, Ohio

Library of Congress Cataloging in Publication Data
Hulse-Killacky, Diana
    Making task groups work in your world / Diana Hulse-Killacky, Jim Killacky,
Jeremiah Donigian.
        p. cm.
    Includes bibliographical references and index.
    ISBN 0-13-906041-3
    1. Small groups.   I. Killacky, Jim.   II. Donigian, Jeremiah.   III. Title

    HM736.H85 2001
    302.3'4—dc21

                                                                    00-028279

Vice President and Publisher: Jeffery W. Johnston
Executive Editor: Kevin M. Davis
Editorial Assistant: Christina M. Kalisch
Development Editor: Heather Doyle Fraser
Production Editor: Linda Hillis Bayma
Copyeditor: Dawn Potter
Design Coordinator: Diane C. Lorenzo
Text Designer: Mia Saunders
Cover Designer: Dan Eckel
Cover art: © SuperStock
Production Manager: Laura Messerly
Electronic Text Management: Marilyn Wilson Phelps, Karen L. Bretz, Melanie N.
    Ortega
Illustrations: Christine Haggerty
Director of Marketing: Kevin Flanagan
Marketing Manager: Amy June
Marketing Services Manager: Krista Groshong

This book was set in Zapf Elliptical by Prentice Hall. It was printed and bound by
R.R. Donnelley & Sons Company. The cover was printed by Phoenix Color Corp.

Quotes appearing on part-opening pages xx, 26, and 112 from John Heider, *The Tao
of Leadership* (Atlanta: Humanics New Age, 1997), pp. 53, 117, 135.

**Copyright © 2001 by Prentice-Hall, Inc., Upper Saddle River, New Jersey
07458.** All rights reserved. Printed in the United States of America. This publication
is protected by Copyright and permission should be obtained from the publisher
prior to any prohibited reproduction, storage in a retrieval system, or transmission in
any form or by any means, electronic, mechanical, photocopying, recording, or likewise. For information regarding permission(s), write to: Rights and Permissions
Department.

10 9 8 7 6 5 4 3 2 1
ISBN: 0-13-906041-3

Foreword

I f we believed all the declarations we hear about our individu-
alistic culture, we might think that most of what gets accomplished is the result of the efforts of individuals working alone.
Nothing, of course, could be further from the truth. Of necessity and often
by choice, much work today is done by groups. On a typical day, most of
us are in one way or another involved in a group project. The range is
wide: from organizing car pools for a soccer team to deciding on an initial
stock price. All of the task groups we work with have certain elements in
common, and to be successful all must meet certain challenges.

If this is so, why has so little attention been paid to the art and science
of task groups? The literature abounds with guidance on leadership,
teams, and the human side of operations management, but sound and
practical advice on how to make task groups work effectively is difficult to
find. *Making Task Groups Work in Your World* fills that void in a way that
is comprehensive yet easy to digest and apply. The secret is the authors'
approach. They have distilled the research on task groups into several
major principles for working with groups and conclude that the most
important is maintaining balance between process and content. Further-
more, they believe that to achieve balance group leaders must attend to
warm-up, action, and closure in each group meeting. To drive home the
importance of learning to apply these principles, the authors use well-con-
structed fictional scenarios to instruct the reader and then offer reflections
on actual case examples to amplify the points.

I particularly appreciate the way the authors continually reinforce the
reader's understanding by reviewing learning points in each chapter and
suggesting points to ponder. Diagrams are used effectively to depict varying elements of warm-up, action, and closure. The authors have honored

the busy lives of their readers by writing a book that can be read in one sitting to learn the major themes and strategies and then returned to again and again as questions and issues arise in readers' own work groups. You will certainly want this book for your own library, but you may want a few extra copies to share with others, particularly with the people who lead the task groups in your world.

Suzanne England
Professor and Dean,
Tulane University School of Social Work

Preface

The annual meeting of the board of the directors of the small-town volunteer rescue squad was scheduled for 7:00 P.M. The meeting usually consisted of two meetings: one in which the outgoing board members were retired and the incoming members voted in; a second in which the new board assumed its position, elected officers, and moved on with the work at hand. At this gathering were some 20 people, including six new board members, five rescue squad volunteers, and nine existing board members (six of whom would be retiring).

During the first meeting, the new board members sat quietly while the others conducted business, going through a lengthy series of annual reports, old business, and the election of the new board. The second meeting finally began at 9:15 P.M. At 9:25 P.M., for the first time that evening, the new members were asked to briefly introduce themselves. One of the new members (who also happens to be a co-author of this book) thought, "This is a terrific example of why people avoid or burn out on public service. Now I know firsthand what we mean by the need for effective task groups." Half a dozen new, enthusiastic, excited, and interested members had arrived to take their place in supporting this vital public service; and by the time their presence was acknowledged, they were tired, the meeting had lasted much later than they had been led to believe, and many of them felt like rubber stamps for a chair who was pushing his agenda as if no one else in the room existed.

Such experiences are all too common in groups, organizations, agencies, schools, and communities across the country. People are bored in meetings, time is wasted, and often nothing seems to get done despite hours of discussion, debate, and sometimes rancorous arguments. We are told that civic responsibility is a thing of the past. People run for local and regional offices on one-issue campaigns that are frequently more exclusionary than inclusionary. In many parts of the country, getting people to run for local or regional elected offices is a daunting task. And while the concepts of community, collaboration, cooperation, and communication are widely trumpeted, their actual practice in our day-to-day community lives is not as common as some yearn for.

Our collective work over the past three decades leads us to offer this book to those who believe that effective task groups can indeed move society in positive directions. Perhaps now more than ever, task groups are a fact of life in volunteer, community, professional, work, political, and educational settings. A central key to their future effectiveness, and therefore to people's willingness to proactively participate and move society forward, is the way they are organized and run, especially given increasing competition for time and commitment to task group activities.

This book is centered around the notion that process (the way we conduct our groups) and content (what we want to achieve) need to be balanced. This balance is attainable if we make the concepts of warm-up, action, and closure the guiding principles for running task groups. To make these concepts come to life, we have drawn together a rich and diverse group of people who share their stories on the application (or lack thereof) of these concepts in a wide range of settings.

In Chapter 1 we present our assumptions about task groups. The chapter also introduces six scenarios with fictional leaders. These situations, drawn from a composite of real-life experiences, are used throughout the book to illuminate various elements of warm-up, action, and closure.

In Chapters 2, 3, and 4, we focus on warm-up, action, and closure. In addition to using the scenarios introduced in Chapter 1, these chapters draw extensively on the words of the contributors. Writing specifically for this book, they share stories from a wide array of task groups to illuminate the value of warm-up, action, and closure in balancing process and content. The contributors write about

- A county-wide coalition for creating a leadership center under the auspices of a community college
- A high school Sophomore Awareness Program
- The committees in a state legislature
- A small business
- A task force of a national association
- An impoverished group in the Philippines
- A college student group focused on ways of undoing racism
- A multi-faith grassroots organization addressing social change
- A nine-county health system agency's executive board
- A children's group focused on school and family concerns

In Chapter 5 we synthesize the major elements of warm-up, action, and closure. We suggest that, in a world in which face-to-face groups are a growing phenomenon, attention to these concepts as ways to balance process and content will leave us with effective groups and, more significantly, increased harmony in society because of the work these groups do.

Chapter 6 revisits the six scenarios introduced in Chapter 1 and offers a plan of action for each situation. Each plan draws from all the elements of warm-up, action, and closure that have been described in previous chapters.

At the end of each chapter, we have included Points to Ponder, which can be used as discussion starters on the material covered in the chapter.

Acknowledgments

On the weekend before a recent annual American Counseling Association's world conference, Diana Hulse-Killacky and Jim Killacky spent a few hours in their New Orleans home developing a detailed outline for this book. Jerry Donigian joined their conversation by phone during the next couple of days. Diana and Jerry met with Merrill/Prentice Hall editor Kevin Davis early during an ACA conference, and by the end they had agreed on a book contract. Thus, a work that we had long discussed and prepared for was launched.

Our distinguished contributors Al Alcazar, Mary Cathcart, Issy Cross, Alice Cryer-Sumler, Mary Frenning, Courtland Lee, John Phillips, Don Reichard, and Larry Stokes have had important roles in the creation of the book. Sam Gladding has been a dear friend and colleague, and his unfailing encouragement and support inspired us at several key points in our work. Our discussions about the book with practicing group leaders in a wide range of settings have resulted in enthusiastic responses. The three of us have developed into an effective task group in the process of writing, rewriting, and rewriting some more. Finally, all those leaders—good, bad, and indifferent—who we have met in our own development may recognize themselves in these pages.

Kurt Kraus, assistant professor of counseling at Shippensburg University, created the figures that depict varying combinations of process and content in warm-up, action, and closure phases of task groups. He was especially creative in designing his drawings to match the scenarios of our fictional leaders.

Finally, thanks to the following reviewers for their comments on the manuscript: Brenda Bova, University of New Mexico; Lynn Bromley, Southern Maine Technical College; Andrew L. Carey, Shippensburg University; Robert K. Conyne, University of Cincinnati; Martha G. Forbes, National Association of Social Workers; Joseph B. Kelley, Pinehurst

School; Malcolm E. Linville, University of Missouri, Kansas City; Sandy Magnuson, Texas Tech University; Vivian L. McCollum, University of New Orleans; Fred B. Newton, Kansas State University; Paul M. Terry, University of Memphis; Herman A. Theeke, Central Michigan University; and Sherman A. Timmins, University of Toledo.

♦

Discover the Companion Website Accompanying This Book

The Prentice Hall Companion Website: A Virtual Learning Environment

Technology is a constantly growing and changing aspect of our field that is creating a need for content and resources. To address this emerging need, Prentice Hall has developed an online learning environment for students and professors alike—Companion Websites—to support our textbooks.

In creating a Companion Website, our goal is to build on and enhance what the textbook already offers. For this reason, the content for each user-friendly website is organized by topic and provides the professor and student with a variety of meaningful resources. Common features of a Companion Website include:

For the Professor—

Every Companion Website integrates **Syllabus Manager**™, an online syllabus creation and management utility.

♦ **Syllabus Manager**™ provides you, the instructor, with an easy, step-by-step process to create and revise syllabi, with direct links into Companion Website and other online content without having to learn HTML.

- Students may logon to your syllabus during any study session. All they need to know is the web address for the Companion Website and the password you've assigned to your syllabus.
- After you have created a syllabus using **Syllabus Manager**™, students may enter the syllabus for their course section from any point in the Companion Website.
- Class dates are highlighted in white and assignment due dates appear in blue. Clicking on a date, the student is shown the list of activities for the assignment. The activities for each assignment are linked directly to actual content, saving time for students.
- Adding assignments consists of clicking on the desired due date, then filling in the details of the assignment—name of the assignment, instructions, and whether or not it is a one-time or repeating assignment.
- In addition, links to other activities can be created easily. If the activity is online, a URL can be entered in the space provided, and it will be linked automatically in the final syllabus.
- Your completed syllabus is hosted on our servers, allowing convenient updates from any computer on the Internet. Changes you make to your syllabus are immediately available to your students at their next logon.

For the Student—

- **Topic Overviews** – outline key concepts in topic areas
- **Electronic Bluebook –** send homework or essays directly to your instructor's email with this paperless form
- **Message Board** – serves as a virtual bulletin board to post–or respond to–questions or comments to/from a national audience
- **Web Destinations** – links to www sites that relate to each topic area
- **Professional Organizations** – links to organizations that relate to topic areas
- **Additional Resources –** access to topic-specific content that enhances material found in the text

To take advantage of these and other resources, please visit the *Making Task Groups Work in Your World* Companion Website at

www.prenhall.com/hulsekillacky

Brief Contents

Contents

MAKING TASK GROUPS
WORK IN YOUR WORLD

◆

PART ONE

INTRODUCTION

◆ ◆ ◆

The wise leader's ability does not rest on
techniques or gimmicks or set exercises.
The method of awareness-of-process
applies to all people and all situations.

◆

This book begins by introducing some common scenarios in the day-to-day operations of ordinary task groups. As you read them, think back to the groups you have led or participated in. Have you ever experienced these moments? Perhaps you were not sure how to convene a group or found that time ran out before the goals were accomplished. Perhaps you noticed that members abruptly got up and left, and you wondered how to end the meeting and make sense of what had transpired. Perhaps members engaged in unpleasant exchanges, and you did not know how to intervene. Maybe you wanted to leave and never come back.

In Chapter 1 we will use these scenarios to illustrate some of our beliefs and assumptions about effective task groups. We will intersperse these assumptions with illustrations of task groups to bring the concepts to life. Our goal is to help you recognize ways to make your task group experiences more enjoyable, productive, and effective.

◆

CHAPTER ONE

Task Groups in Our Everyday Lives

◆

Paul started a landscaping business several years ago. Because of increased demand, he has hired six new staff members who have lots of ideas and energy. Paul plans to bring all of them together so they can meet one another and develop a sense of teamwork. He wants to harness their energy and excitement while making sure that everyone works for the good of the business. Some members seem open to the idea of group meetings, while others just want to do their job and avoid what they perceive as "touchy-feely" time. Paul is determined to host this group in a few weeks and wonders how to make his team-building effort useful and satisfying for everyone.

◆ ◆ ◆

The Reverend Marvin Ellison has called together local church members for their first fall meeting, scheduled for 7:00 to 8:30 P.M. Some members arrive on time, others late; so he begins about 7:15. He has an agenda, but conversation centers on other issues. Several members tell the new music minister all about church politics; another, who chairs the education committee, critiques a new restaurant in town. The structured part of the meeting finally gets underway with a few reports mingled with interruptions, especially from several vocal members of the council. As 8:30 approaches, only a few items on the agenda have been addressed. Several mem-

bers observe, "I thought this meeting was over at 8:30. I have other things to do." There is much shifting in chairs as people check the clock and pack up their materials. Reverend Ellison has not addressed the pacing and timing of the evening session and has not checked with members to see if it is okay to extend the meeting time.

Letitia has just been elected to the education subcommittee of the state legislature. This subcommittee is comprised of members of both major political parties. Although it is early in the legislative session and the subcommittee has only met a few times, she has been happy with how members have addressed various tasks and at the friendly nature of the exchanges during their deliberations. At this particular meeting members are charged with making budget decisions, but for some reason other topics have taken priority. Just as Letitia realizes that there are only 15 minutes left in the meeting, several restless members start looking at their watches. One states, "I've got to go now; I forgot to tell you that I have another meeting across the street." Another jumps up: "Oh, I have to meet Representative Smith in a few minutes. . . . Gotta run." Letitia feels a sense of dread. The task is not complete, and these members are leaving without discussing how they plan to help make these looming budget decisions.

Jane is the new president of a local professional organization with a membership encompassing different races, ethnicities, ages, sexual orientations, and genders. She is presiding over a monthly board meeting in which budget issues are being discussed. This topic sets off strong disagreements. When an older lesbian board member expresses her viewpoint about making sure money is allocated to support the needs of gay and lesbian youth in the area, several members start screaming at her. She continues to push her point, while others loudly express their different convictions. Jane becomes overwhelmed and cannot create order. She adjourns the meeting.

◆ ◆ ◆

Richard is the chair of the English department at a large high school. At the beginning of the school year he calls a teachers' meeting to discuss how to implement a state-mandated English program. By the end of the first 20 minutes, it becomes apparent that three first-year teachers who have recently graduated from well-respected teacher education programs are intent on presenting their ideas from current research literature. Older teachers, unhappy with their new colleagues, find these ideas unrealistic. One responds, "I remember we tried a similar idea 16 years ago, and it didn't work." This teacher then begins a detailed story about the history of the high school's English program. Richard looks around the room at signs of verbal and nonverbal dissatisfaction. He knows that if the different viewpoints and perspectives are not quickly addressed and integrated, the teaching team will be ineffective or fall apart.

Maria has been asked by the town council to facilitate several meetings for the local community recreation committee. The purpose of this evening's meeting is to begin discussions about a location for the new community playground. Maria knows who the committee members are and recognizes that some people are opinionated and like to talk, while others are quieter and more reflective. She wants to make sure that members stay on task and that everyone's ideas are included. She wonders if she can help create a setting in which all members can contribute to the task in meaningful ways.

These scenarios represent common occurrences in the lives of ordinary individuals in business, school, community, health care, church, political, and other settings in which people come together to complete tasks and solve problems. Often they gather without professional resources, huge budgets, or much time. For the most part, these individuals have not had formal training in group work, nor are they aware of the kinds of leadership tasks and personal issues that need to be addressed to make groups useful, enjoyable, and productive within the limits of time and available resources.

Groups in the 20th Century

One of the most interesting phenomena of the 20th century has been the growth, development, and presence of group work. From the earliest formal groups, such as Pratt's psychotherapy group for patients with tuberculosis in the early 1900s, to more recent self-help and cooperative learning groups, we have witnessed the emergence of a massive array of groups, from therapy settings to boardrooms.

From the beginning there was a certain tension among proponents of group work and those who believed that groups diminished individuality. Throughout this century group work has often been considered a liability. For example, in the 1960s and early 1970s many groups were led by people who had little or no experience working effectively with group dynamics and personal feelings. The unfortunate outcomes damaged positive views of group work. However, professional group associations such as the National Training Laboratory (NTL) and the Association for Specialists in Group Work (ASGW) and the development of training standards and rigorous research initiatives have helped group work develop an image of a sound professional practice (Gladding, 1999).

There is a network of systems and organizational development concerned primarily with businesses and large organizations that brings in trainers to prepare group facilitators. Nevertheless, people still tell us that they need help in local situations—those common, everyday occurrences not covered by corporate training.

Successful groups, characterized by accomplishment and personal satisfaction, are those in which people

◆ Feel listened to

◆ Are accepted for their individuality

◆ Have a voice

◆ Are part of a climate in which leaders and members acknowledge and appreciate varied perspectives, needs, and concerns

◆ Understand and support the purpose of the group

◆ Have the opportunity to contribute to the accomplishment of particular tasks

Although these goals are not easy to attain, they are possible to learn. Using everyday language, this book explains the concepts and principles that can help people like you lead task groups in community, business, political, and educational settings.

During the past 20 years we have witnessed a growing number of groups, particularly task groups. The Association for Specialists in Group Work (1992) has approved a set of training standards that defines task/work groups as those including "task forces, committees, planning groups, community organizations, discussion groups, study circles, and learning groups" (p. 13). It is often cost-effective to meet in groups; and when groups work well, the combination of many voices enhances the likelihood of successful outcomes. This is why we do things in groups: because the power of the collective is greater than the individual. Too often, however, we lose sight of that positive attribute of group work. Effective leaders are those who understand how to engage and use the power of the group to accomplish tasks.

Childers and Couch (1989) have documented a number of misconceptions people have about group counseling, which can also be applied to task groups. Three that seem particularly relevant here are (1) groups force people to lose their identity, (2) you have to spill your guts in a group, and (3) all groups are touchy-feely. For example, in considering the scenario about Paul, who wishes to create a work team at his landscaping business, we see immediately that he needs to address the misconception that a team-building group must be touchy-feely. Just the sight of chairs set in a circle can prompt individuals to bolt from a room, crying, "I'm not interested in that group stuff!" Such ingrained reactions are the result of unfortunate experiences, misrepresentations of group work, poor leadership, and media influence. Whatever the cause, leaders should expect that members of task groups will bring with them certain negative beliefs and misconceptions about the idea of being in a group. It is a leader's job to anticipate these reactions, address them, and model behaviors that convince members that groups are useful ways to spend time and accomplish tasks.

Effective group work can make major and valuable contributions to task initiatives. It has become clear, however, that certain themes run through all groups regardless of purpose or focus (Conyne, Wilson, & Ward, 1997; Donigian & Malnati, 1997; Kraus & Hulse-Killacky, 1996). In task groups these themes are process and content. The challenge is to strike a balance between these themes so that the goals of the group can be attained.

Despite certain similarities, all group situations are not the same. A corporate board meeting is different from a volunteer group designed to respond to the needs of homeless people in the community. Differences in composition, experience, longevity, and purpose create situations that require varied strategies. Nevertheless, there are three major phases common to all task groups: *warm-up,* which refers to good planning; *action,* which refers to performance; and *closure,* which refers to how the group ends and how members reflect on their work in the group (Conyne et al., 1997).

Small groups have emerged as a powerful tool to assist people in building and shaping collaborative and cooperative climates. They are an increasingly popular vehicle for solving problems and addressing a variety of issues in the work, social, community, educational, and business arenas. One great challenge for participants is learning to understand and respect differences while consciously attending to the basic humanity that binds us together. An atmosphere of safety and trust is enhanced through activities that bring people together and help them learn about their similarities and differences. This focus is important because no matter what the group purpose or theme may be, similarities and differences among members play a key role in the group's success or failure.

Ingredients for Effective Task Groups

We now turn to some assumptions that underlie our conceptual framework for leading groups. We apply these assumptions to all groups, believing that adherence to them will make any group work better. To simplify our discussion, we use the term *leader* to refer to a committee chair, a facilitator, a convenor, or a presider of meetings.

The assumptions are

- A clear purpose exists
- Balancing process and content issues
- Supporting process and content in all subsystems
- Building a culture that appreciates differences
- Developing an ethic of cooperation, collaboration, and mutual respect
- Addressing conflict
- Exchanging feedback
- Addressing here-and-now issues in the group
- Inviting members to be active resources
- Developing members' ability to be influential
- Practicing effective leadership skills
- Allowing members time to reflect on their work

A Clear Purpose Exists

Let's return to Paul and his desire for team building among his landscaping staff. Recall that some workers support his idea, while others do not. Paul needs to be very clear about the purpose of these meetings and remain sensitive to the fact that multiple individual needs will always be present. He may find that presenting a general theme of team building at the meeting will not be enough; the concept may not be clear or precise enough for his staff members. Paul will enhance his chances of success by sending out an agenda ahead of time. And at the beginning of the group, he must immediately engage all members in a discussion about defining the group's purpose. Thus, he will set in motion the forces for building a culture—for developing a spirit of cooperation, collaboration, and community. His goal is to enlist everyone's input.

We have learned through experience that groups work best when the purpose is clear to all participants. This assumption requires the leader to address both group and individual goals and to articulate and keep track of the group's purpose. A leader must be able to walk a fine line between working with members to clarify group goals and negotiating the various individual goals that surface.

Balancing Process and Content Issues

Groups must focus on both the content (or purpose) and on the process— that is, how things happen in a group and how members participate. Leaders can use two sets of questions to guide their work.

Attend to process by considering the following questions:

- Who am I?
- Who am I with you?
- Who are we together?

Content questions include

- What do we have to do?
- What do we need to do to accomplish our goals?

Both sets of questions are important. However, in many task groups the content focus predominates, resulting in little or no attention to how members and leaders relate to one another. Reflect on Maria's upcoming meeting with the local community recreation committee. She must emphasize both sets of questions. Because she is already concerned about a potential imbalance in verbal participation, she may enhance her chances for success by first taking time to help people get acquainted—to orient themselves to the purpose of the group and to one another (Conyne, 1989). The group work literature is full of references to the leader's responsibility for attending to human relations issues if the group is to be successful (see Conyne, 1989; Gladding, 1999; Lyman, 1993). As Sam Gladding has observed, "anyone who believes a meeting is run by information and facts needs to revisit what is happening in the group. Time after time I realized it was relationships between group members that either made or unmade the productivity in groups I led or in which I participated" (cited in Campbell, 1996, p.74). If process and content are given equal importance—that is, balanced—the work of the group will be greatly enhanced.

Supporting Process and Content in All Subsystems

Groups have several subsystems, including the leader, the members, and subsets of members. Leaders can strengthen the productive work of any group by attending to these subsystems and the interactions between several or more subsystems (Donigian & Malnati, 1997). For example, both leaders and participants must observe what is being said and how it is being said. In considering the scenario about Richard's teachers' meeting, we see that Richard has already begun to observe the growing dissatisfaction of certain members as they listen to a veteran teacher present historical data about the English department. Richard is aware that some members are tuning out and that a breakdown in communication is occurring among members. In addition, he is slowly losing his ability to exert any control over the group. As a preventive measure, Richard might anticipate these differences of viewpoint. First, he can invite teachers to describe themselves individually and explain what each brings to the task of implementing the state-mandated English program. By stopping occasionally to see that everyone is paying attention and understanding what has transpired thus far, he will be able to identify problems before they become overwhelming.

Time for Building a Culture That Appreciates Differences

Groups work best when time is taken for culture building and learning about differences. Multiple perspectives always exist when people gather in groups (Pederson, 1994). These perspectives might relate to race, culture, ethnicity, religion, gender, age, sexual orientation, or disability status. They may also surface in the form of work style preferences. Examples include preferences for thinking and pondering rather than immediately verbalizing thoughts, preferences for getting a job done quickly versus keeping options open for further discussion and analysis, and preferences for defined structure versus openness to ambiguity and spontaneity. Such differences can be a rich resource in a group; conversely, they can create discord. Culture building, then, means developing guidelines for tolerating such differences within the group. The leader can help members develop empathy for differences by giving members time up front to learn about each other.

Consider the disruption in Jane's board meeting. Recall that she is a new president of an organization that needs to make budget decisions. Members arrive with strong and diverse viewpoints and priorities. But has Jane taken time to help members become acquainted? Have they asked one another, "Who am I?" "Who am I with you?" and "Who are we together?" Has she addressed the tension between group goals and individual goals?

As noted, differences can be sources of positive or destructive energy. We have discovered, however, that when people are given time to learn about each other, they enhance their ability to understand and appreciate different world views. Such empathy cannot be developed if time is not devoted to exploring these differences. Certainly, in task groups time is usually at a premium, making leaders reluctant to undertake process explorations. But we believe they have no choice if they want to develop a successful group. Members want to know "Can I be myself and still be a member of this group?" Groups need to know who their members really are and be open to moving beyond what Frew (1986) calls the "illusion of inclusion"—when members perceive that their connections to others are tied only to similarities. Leaders must help members learn who they are in relation to others and how multiple perspectives and styles can be used to enhance rather than hinder their work.

Developing an Ethic of Cooperation, Collaboration, and Mutual Respect

Many educators and leaders in organizational development believe that collaboration, cooperation, and mutual respect are necessary in our changing, fast-paced, and complex world (Astin, 1987; Palmer, 1987; Schindler-Rainman, 1981; Whipple, 1987). Others (for example, Ettin, 1993) believe that, as people learn to cooperate and collaborate in small groups, they can become more effective citizens in other areas of life. The task of creating and maintaining collaborative environments is not easy and requires a foundation of effective, open, and honest communication. In task groups the content or product often obscures personal and interpersonal arenas. Yet a focus on process allows people to begin a journey toward genuine understanding, respect, and empathy for different world views, styles, and needs. Ultimately, these actions foster the development of a community of people who can work together. Therefore, leaders must attend to the relationships in the group with the same intensity and enthusiasm they give to the content. In many cases task groups may achieve their goal without any attention to the group process. Frequently, however, members leave such situations with no desire for future group activity.

In Jane's budget meeting and Richard's teachers' meeting, each leader could reduce further disruption by giving members a structure for articulating their needs and perspectives while encouraging them to listen to the viewpoints of others. Providing such a structure can be an effective step in recognizing and understanding differing points of view. People do not have to agree with one another to work in harmony; however, they need time to learn who the other players are. Otherwise, they will develop their own opinions of others, often based on inaccurate or inadequate information. The goal is not a homogenous grouping; rather, it is to understand and respect the various positions and skills that different viewpoints can bring to a task group.

Addressing Conflict

Whenever two or more people come together, the potential for conflict exists. Even though conflict is natural in all groups, it makes many people uncomfortable (Donigian & Malnati, 1997; Hulse-Killacky & Page, 1994). Issues that generate conflict include authority, autonomy, attraction, change, power, control, and dependence. These issues may affect leaders as well as members. "The difference is that the leader has to . . . come to terms with issues that generate conflict" (Donigian & Malnati, 1997, p. 6). Otherwise, the leader will not be able to effectively help group members work through conflict when it occurs.

Whitaker and Lieberman (1964) developed the focal conflict model to conceptualize the conflict process (see Figure 1.1). *Disturbing motives* are a member's private agenda, wishes, desires, or secrets, which conflict with his *reactive motives* (or fears), such as ridicule, embarrassment, and exclusion.[1] In other words, he might want to reveal his disturbing motive, while fearing laughter, rejection, ridicule, or some other distressing consequence. The conflict between the disturbing motive and the reactive motive generates anxiety in the member. Because people usually cannot tolerate anxiety for long, he will likely adopt a solution to relieve it. As Figure 1.1 shows, this solution may take one of two forms: *restrictive* or *enabling*.

---

1.   Our use of pronouns alternates between male and female to ensure the flow of inclusive language.

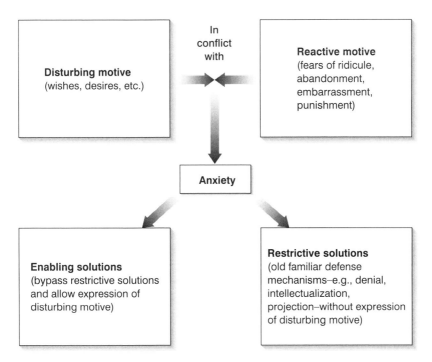

FIGURE 1.1
Focal conflict model
Source: From *Systemic Group Therapy: A Triadic Model* by J. Donigian and R. Malnati. © 1997. Reprinted with permission of Wadsworth Publishing, a division of Thomson Learning. Fax (800) 730-2215.

Restrictive solutions are a member's defense mechanisms. Faced with intolerable anxiety, the member will resort to familiar solutions such as intellectualization, denial or projection. These restrictive solutions are designed to relieve the member's anxiety as well as reduce the member's projected motives or fears. Consequently, resorting to a restrictive solution precludes verbal expression of the disturbing motive. In contrast, an enabling solution bypasses the member's reactive fear and allows at least some expression of the disturbing motive. The focal conflict model can also be applied to the leader and group behavior. For instance, the leader who wishes to reveal personal feelings regarding the behavior of a group member or of the whole group (disturbing motive) may be too fearful of the member's or the group's disapproval to do so (reactive motive). The leader, then, adopts a restrictive solution to relieve the anxiety engendered by holding simultaneously disturbing and reactive motives. (Donigian & Malnati, 1997, pp. 7–8)

We can use Reverend Ellison's church group to illustrate the focal conflict model. Although Reverend Ellison comes to the meeting with an agenda, individual members often break away from it to discuss other matters. The group as a whole is not addressing the agenda, while the Reverend is wrapped up in self-talk about whether or not all the agenda items will be addressed. For example, he does not check with members to see if it is okay to extend the meeting time.

In the scenario he hears from two members, who are engaging in restrictive solutions in response to the agenda. If they had stated up front their concerns about the agenda (perhaps "I think the agenda is too long" or "I think there are too many irrelevant items" or "I have some items I'd like to add to the agenda"), they would have verbalized their disturbing motives and thus engaged in enabling solutions. Instead, they allowed their reactive motives to dominate, which led to restrictive solutions such as critiquing a new restaurant and discussing church politics.

The group as a whole also engages in restrictive solutions. Not only is the agenda not addressed, but the group tolerates interruptions and thus avoids the agenda. If the group had disclosed its disturbing motive about the agenda and the interruptions, it would have engaged in an enabling solution. Then the meeting time might have been used more productively.

The Reverend also employs restrictive solutions. If he had mentioned his concern about completing the agenda, he would not only have revealed his disturbing motive but also employed an enabling solution. Instead, he may think, "If I say that I want the group to address the agenda, members will reject me or think I'm a fool"—a reactive motive.

The focal conflict model helps us understand the behavior of the group as a whole, group members, and the leader. It establishes that all relationships are interdependent. These relationships include member to member, leader to member, member to leader, leader to group, member(s) to group, group to leader, and group to member(s).

Exchanging Feedback

Feedback, like conflict, can make group members uncomfortable. Research on feedback in small groups reveals that both leaders and members need to make feedback clear, immediate, to the point, and behavioral (see Jacobs, Jacobs, Feldman, & Cavior, 1973; Kaul & Bednar, 1986; Morran, Robison, & Stockton, 1985; Morran & Stockton, 1980). However, the process of giving and receiving feedback is complex. Yalom (1983) reveals how difficult giving feedback can be, observing that "group members do not engage in the process of feedback naturally and spontaneously. Feedback is not a commonplace transaction" (p. 187). Stating differing views, giving and receiving corrective feedback, and managing the conflict that is inevitable when people come together in groups are critical tasks for leaders and members. As group members develop the ability to effectively address these process issues, they can recognize and work through blockages that occur in task groups. If a goal is to promote environments in which group participants can address pluralism, cultural diversity, and multiple viewpoints, then working with conflict and feedback is a necessary step.

All of the leaders in our scenarios should heed these suggestions. For example, Reverend Ellison might demonstrate how to give feedback by cutting off extraneous conversations. He can model his own openness to receiving feedback by admitting that he had not checked with members about extending the meeting time. Then he can ask for member input.

Maria can invite committee members to give feedback about how the meeting is progressing. Because she is conscious that some people talk more easily than others, she can work to maintain a climate of equality by making sure that everyone has a voice.

Paul can model his openness to listening to differing staff viewpoints about the team-building session. At the same time he can work with them to make their time together useful and productive.

Jane, who is facing an explosive situation, can stop the action and negotiate a healthier structure for providing feedback and expressing disagreement with ideas.

Addressing Here-and-Now Issues in the Group

Groups work best when leaders and members recognize what is happening right now. Because group attention is often devoted to content, leaders may not notice potentially distracting behaviors. Attention to the here-and-now is critical for helping members accomplish their goals and remove blockages to their work (Conyne, 1989). Heider (1997) suggests: "The wise leader knows what is happening in a group by being aware of what is happening here and now. By staying present and aware of what is happening, the leader can do less yet achieve more" (p. 93). In other words, by focusing exclusively on content, agendas, and other cognitive issues, the leader cannot observe and comment on what is actually occurring in the moment. She needs to be flexible, concentrating on both content and process.

Letitia's legislative group, Richard's teachers' meeting, and Reverend Ellison's church meeting all have different content issues. In all cases, however, attention to the here-and-now can be a powerful tool for avoiding trouble. If leaders are aware of various nonverbal gestures, they can name them. Thus, the "elephant" in the room is identified rather than ignored. Simply saying, "I'd like to stop for a moment and check in with everyone to see how things are going in the group," allows for a pause that may invite feedback that can then be addressed. Such a statement can begin a dialogue that helps group members identify forces such as traffic jams, sick family members, and headaches that may be hindering the productivity of the group's work, thus freeing up energy to focus on the work at hand. Letitia can discover that her subcommittee will not be able to finish its agenda at this meeting and can enlist help in deciding what steps to take before members begin leaving. Richard's observations can help teachers recognize their differences and explore how to use them in service of group goals. Reverend Ellison can learn more about the meeting's haphazard progress and be able to stop and realign the goals and decide what can be realistically accomplished in the remaining time.

Inviting Members to Be Active Resources

"Successful groups are those in which the leader or leaders can work together with group members to design the group effectively, to design the environment successfully, to figure out where it's going" (Conyne, cited in Ward, 1993, p. 102). Leaders must let members know quickly and clearly that their input and contribution are vital to the success of the group. As products of educational systems in which we have been conditioned to sit in rows and respond only when invited, many of us find this shift challenging. It is clear, however, that when members have a voice, task groups become more productive and dynamic; and group members learn skills that they can transfer to other groups.

All of our scenario leaders need to think of ways to enlist members' voices to achieve group goals and to reduce the pressure on the leader to do all the work. The challenge here is to take time to engage members and help them believe that their individual and collective input is important to the group effort.

Developing Members' Ability to Be Influential

Here we emphasize the notion of the leader as both leader and follower. If an individual can both lead and follow, then the familiar "I must be on top to be in charge" view can be replaced by "I can be in charge and part of the group." This shift allows a spirit of mutuality and interdependence to surface and thrive in the group. Leaders must engage all members rather than impose their own favorite viewpoints, agendas, or structures. Leadership then becomes a shared experience in which all participants work together in service of the group endeavor. When leaders help members learn effective skills, then all groups become more satisfying and productive.

Our scenario leaders need to examine their own perspectives about leadership and be comfortable with extending their power and influence to members. Do these leaders really believe that members are just as important to the success of a group? Positive critical reflection on this question can allow leaders to discover ways of genuinely engaging members.

Practicing Effective Leadership Skills

In a pioneering study, Lieberman, Yalom, and Miles (1973) examined the types of leadership characteristics associated with successful groups. Their analysis yielded four factors:

1. *Caring.* Leaders recognize and acknowledge the needs of the group and group members.
2. *Meaning attribution.* Leaders help members understand their work and their worth in the group.
3. *Emotional stimulation.* Leaders acknowledge members' emotional connection to each other and the issues at hand.
4. *Executive function.* Leaders demonstrate ability and skill in managing timing and pacing and keeping the group on task and moving forward.

While traditionally associated with counseling, support, personal growth, and therapy groups, these skills are also important in task groups (Conyne et al., 1997) and are significant aides in balancing process and content.

When leaders are high in caring, they present themselves as authentic, approachable, and accessible people who can help the group set guidelines for positive outcomes. Caring is especially important for Paul as he tries to enlist the participation of his landscaping staff—both those who agree with the group idea and those who do not.

Meaning attribution occurs when leaders provide explanations, clarify and interpret what is going on, and generally help members apply meaning and purpose to what they are experiencing in the group. In Letitia's subcommittee, Reverend Ellison's church group, and Jane's budget meeting, all three leaders can use meaning attribution to assess members' thoughts and behaviors as they relate to the group's work. Meaning attribution is enhanced by simply stopping and summarizing the content of what has transpired, thereby helping members see where they have been and where they might be going.

Emotional stimulation involves helping members share their thoughts and feelings about the issue under discussion and understand how their way of communicating affects the work of the group. Leaders who use emotional stimulation are viewed positively by members because people tend to have strong feelings about certain topics, as evidenced in Jane's budget meeting and Richard's teachers' meeting. For example, by inviting the veteran teacher to clarify his frustration with new ideas, Richard can model the effective use of moderate emotional stimulation in a task group.

Finally, executive function, in moderate amounts, is essential for successful group experiences. Groups need to have a clear beginning and ending; leaders need a range of skills such as managing time, pacing, sequencing, summarizing, clarifying, cutting off, drawing out, and holding and shifting the focus (Jacobs, Masson, & Harvill, 1998). These skills are essential for helping task groups move through their various agendas in a timely and efficient manner. Both Letitia and Reverend Ellison could practice executive function skills more effectively. In each case the leaders came to points in their meetings where time had run out, and they were faced with unhappy members who simply got up and left without sufficient closure.

Allowing Members Time to Reflect on Their Work

Heider (1997) believes that time for reflection is crucial: "Allow regular time for silent reflection. Turn inward and digest what has happened. Let the senses rest and grow still. When group members have time to reflect, they can see more clearly what is essential in themselves and others" (p. 23).

When leaders and members take time to reflect on what is happening—both in terms of content (achieving the goals of the group) and process (recognizing how things happen in the group)—then all participants can better understand and appreciate the work of the group. Helping members understand the meaning of their work together is a tricky issue and is often sacrificed in task groups. Racing through agendas and trying to meet goals and deadlines do not allow for reflection and closure. Donigian and Malnati (1997), however, invite leaders to provide opportunities for members to reflect on individual and group learning. Such time helps all participants connect their work to their subsequent responsibilities and therefore helps all members determine what the next steps might be.

A process observer is an important tool for helping members reflect on the work of the group. Process observers serve as the conscience of the group. Their primary role is to help the task group pay attention to how members are interacting and how they are addressing the work of the group. In addition, process observers can illuminate instances in which group members may be avoiding conflict. The process observer, then, can be a great resource for the task group leader. If the leader experiences an impasse or a work blockage, he can ask the process observer to give feedback on why or how the group is stuck. All members of the group should understand the role and functions of the process observer, and it is best that this person not be a working member. By being an outsider, she can provide critical feedback and reflection without being embroiled in the complex interactions.

This advice is important for Letitia's legislative group and Reverend Ellison's church group. Without some reflection and summary, certain members will leave abruptly; and both leaders and the remaining members will be unclear about each member's contributions to upcoming events. Reflection may be a hard goal to address in a task group, but it is essential for making sure that everyone is working for the group's best interests. Leaders can stop the group, even when unexpected departures occur, and ask each member to provide some information about what he will do before the next meeting. This action is crucial if there is to be useful continuity between one meeting and the next. Otherwise, meetings may end but really not end: the next meeting will seem like a vague extension of the previous one, and ambiguity will prevail.

The following vignette illustrates how approaches to warm-up, action, and closure can influence a group's work.

Bringing Warm-up, Action, and Closure to Life in the First Meeting of a Graduate Course

Warm-up

In preparation for an intensive one-week course on group work, the instructor met for three hours on the preceding Saturday morning with 20 graduate students and her team of advanced students whose duties were to co-lead small groups during the week and serve as process observers for the class sessions.

At this meeting the instructor made a few introductory comments about the purpose of the class and the importance of developing a learning culture that would invite participation from all members and would convey an appreciation of the many resources that each student brought to the class. She acknowledged that the morning's activities would focus primarily on helping members to begin answering the questions "who am I?" "who am I with you?" and "is the class purpose clear?" She said that the focus on human relations issues would provide a foundation for the collective work of all class members during the coming week.

The instructor began with a names activity: all members were asked to give their first name, state how they got their name, tell if they liked it, and, if not, explain what they would change it to. She started the round to model the activity. After completing the round, she asked members to state their first names again; then she asked them to try and say everyone's name. After a few tries, several class members actually stated everyone's first name. At this point the instructor asked the class to tell her what they thought the purpose of the activity was and what meaning it had for them in the context of the class setting. Responses were quick: several observed that by telling a bit about their names, everyone was learning something about every other member. Others noted that the brief scenarios associated with names helped them to remember names. Still others commented that the activity helped them feel more at ease, and they appreciated the opportunity to feel connected to others through the simple task of learning names.

Action

The instructor took the time to help members reflect on the meaning of what had happened and to emphasize once again that the name exercise was linked to the interpersonal learning that would have direct bearing on future events in the class. She then walked the members through several more activities. Members were asked to move around the room according to their position on preferences such as talking things out versus thinking things through; liking the big picture versus wanting the specific details; making decisions based on logical implications versus knowing the impact that a decision has on others; and coming to a conclusion and finishing a task versus staying open to more discussion of options. As these positions and others were visualized and discussed, members identified how their own styles were similar to and different from others in the class. As the instructor helped members think through the implications of these styles, members began to see how such knowledge could help them develop understanding and respect for other views. They also recognized that the presence of differing styles could be resources for the class work.

Another activity centered on expectations for the class experience. Members were asked to write down their expectations of themselves, their expectations of their classmates, and their expectations of the instructor. In small groups and then in the larger group, members discussed their responses. Expectations were clarified about what the class time would entail, what they could expect, and what was expected of them. Through discussion, members began to recognize how their needs and expectations were similar to and different from others in the class. This activity was connected to the next one in which members were asked to develop some consensus statements about class attendance and participation. When everyone felt comfortable with the statements, they gave a visual thumbs-up sign, and the instructor agreed to type the statements and hand them out at the next class. The typed statements would serve as guidelines for how the class as a whole would conduct its business. Next, the syllabus readings and assignments were reviewed.

Closure

The process observers offered commentaries on what they had seen during the morning session. They discussed events that were directly related to process issues and those related to content and purpose. The observers indicated that they would have a written statement of their observations for class members at the next meeting. Finally, the instructor led the class in a closing round. Members were asked to reflect on what had happened during the morning session and what they would take with them. Reflection time was again employed as the group prepared to end and each member had an opportunity to speak.

Summary of Part One

We have presented a number of assumptions with illustrations that, when summarized, can form a series of "if . . . then" statements. These statements are the philosophical basis of our model of warm-up, action, and closure in task groups. A good model should not be used to impose on members; rather, it should serve as a practical guide for designing, beginning, implementing, maintaining, and ending effective group experiences. A good model, therefore, can provide direction for a single session group or a group over time and can be adapted in many ways, depending on the purpose of the group and the special needs of the members, the leader, and the group as a whole.

If the purpose of the group is clear to all participants,

If process and content issues are balanced,

If the systems of group as a whole, leader, member, and subsets of members are recognized and acknowledged,

If time is taken for culture building and learning about each other,

If the ethic of collaboration, cooperation, and mutual respect is developed and nurtured,

If conflict is addressed,

If feedback is exchanged,

If leaders pay attention to the here-and-now,

If members are active resources,

If members learn to be effective and influential participants,

If leaders exhibit a range of skills for helping members address task and human relations issues,

If members and leaders take time to reflect on what is happening,

Then the goals of the group through cooperation, collaboration, and community building will be achieved, and task groups of all types will likely be successful, enjoyable, productive, and effective experiences for members and leaders alike.

◆ ◆ ◆

Points to Ponder

1. Explain why leaders delineate a clear purpose for forming their task groups.

2. Explain the difference between process and content.

3. Explain why leaders need to balance process and content.

4. Leaders can begin to differentiate between content and process by answering three process questions and two content questions. Present them and discuss why they can be helpful.

5. Explain what is meant by group culture. Explain the significance of group culture in developing a task group.

6. Explain how cooperation, collaboration, and mutual respect relate to process concerns.

7. Explain how disturbing motive, reactive motive, restrictive solution, and enabling solution are related to conflict resolution.

8. Explain why the here-and-now focus is useful.

9. Recall and discuss the four leadership skills that all effective group leaders need to practice.

◆ ◆ ◆

References

Association for Specialists in Group Work (1992). Professional standards for the training of group workers. *Journal for Specialists in Group Work, 17,* 12–19.

Astin, A. (1987). Competition or cooperation? Teaching teamwork as a basic skill. *Change, 19,* 12–19.

Campbell, L. (1996). Samuel T. Gladding: A sense of self in the group. *Journal for Specialists in Group Work, 21,* 69–80.

Childers, J. H., Jr., & Couch, R. D. (1989). Myths about group counseling: Identifying and challenging misconceptions. *Journal for Specialists in Group Work, 14,* 105–111.

Conyne, R. K. (1989). *How personal growth and task groups work.* Newbury Park, CA: Sage.

Conyne, R. K., Wilson, F. R., & Ward, D. E. (1997). *Comprehensive group work: What it means and how to teach it.* Alexandria, VA: American Counseling Association.

Donigian, J., & Malnati, R. (1997). *Systemic group therapy: A triadic model.* Pacific Grove, CA: Brooks/Cole.

Ettin, M. F. (1993). Links between group process and social, political, and cultural issues. In H. I. Kaplan & B. J. Sadock (Eds.), *Comprehensive group psychotherapy* (3rd ed., pp. 699–716). Baltimore: Williams & Wilkins.

Frew, J. E. (1986). Leadership approaches to achieve maximum therapeutic potential in mutual groups. *Journal for Specialists in Group Work, 11,* 93–99.

Gladding, S. T. (1999). *Group work: A counseling specialty* (3rd ed.). Upper Saddle River, NJ: Merrill/Prentice Hall.

Heider, J. (1997). *The tao of leadership.* Atlanta: Humanics New Age.

Hulse-Killacky, D., & Page, B. J. (1994). Development of the Corrective Feedback Instrument: A tool for use in counselor training groups. *Journal for Specialists in Group Work, 19,* 197–210.

Jacobs, M., Jacobs, A., Feldman, G., & Cavior, N. (1973). Feedback II—the "credibility gap": Delivery of positive and negative and emotional and behavioral feedback in groups. *Journal of Consulting and Clinical Psychology, 41,* 215–223.

Jacobs, E. E., Masson, R. L., & Harvill, R. L. (1998). *Group counseling: Strategies and skills* (3rd ed.). Pacific Grove, CA: Brooks/Cole.

Kaul, T. J., & Bednar, R. L. (1986). Experiential group research: Results, questions, and suggestions. In S. L. Garfield & A. Bergin (Eds.), *Handbook of psychotherapy and behavior change* (2nd ed., pp. 671–714). New York: Wiley.

Kraus, K., & Hulse-Killacky, D. (1996). Balancing process and content in groups: A metaphor. *Journal for Specialists in Group Work, 21,* 90–93.

Lieberman, M., Yalom, I., & Miles, M. (1973). *Encounter groups: First facts.* New York: Basic Books.

Lyman, L. (1993). Group building for successful inclusion programs. Paper presented at the Flint Hills Educational Research Development Association Special Education Inclusion Conference. (ERIC Document Reproduction Service No. ED 366 138)

Morran, D. K., Robison, F. F., & Stockton, R. (1985). Feedback exchange in counseling groups: An analysis of message content and receiver acceptance as a function of leader versus member delivery, session, and valence. *Journal of Counseling Psychology, 32,* 57-67.

Morran, D. K., & Stockton, R. (1980). Effect of self-concept on group member reception of positive and negative feedback. *Journal of Counseling Psychology, 27,* 260–267.

Palmer, P. (1987). Community, conflict and ways of knowing: Ways to deepen our educational agenda. *Change, 19,* 20–25.

Pederson, P. (1994). *A handbook for developing multicultural awareness* (2nd ed.). Alexandria, VA: American Counseling Association.

Schindler-Rainman, E. (1981). Training task-group leaders. *Journal for Specialists in Group Work, 6,* 171–174.

Ward, D. (1993). An interview with Bob Conyne. *Journal for Specialists in Group Work, 18,* 99–108.

Whipple, W. R. (1987). Collaborative learning: Recognizing it when we see it. *Bulletin of the American Association of Higher Education,* pp. 3–7.

Whitaker, D. S., & Lieberman, M. (1964). *Psychotherapy through the group process.* New York: Atherton Press.

Yalom, I. D. (1983). *Inpatient group psychotherapy.* New York: Basic Books.

◆

PART TWO

A MODEL FOR TASK GROUPS

◆ ◆ ◆

If you are aware of what is happening
and how things happen, you can act
accordingly. You can steer clear of
trouble, and be both vital and effective.

◆

n Part 2 we present our model for task groups. The goal of the visual conceptual model is balance between process and content. Too much focus on content obscures attention to human relations issues and the development of cooperation, collaboration, and community among all participants. Conversely, too much attention to process, especially process that is not effectively and clearly linked to content, hinders the group's ability to address important task and purpose issues. When process is addressed without a clear connection to the group's purpose, members often become frustrated and begin to associate process with irrelevant, unnecessary, and tangential events (Conyne, 1989; Kraus & Hulse-Killacky, 1996; Ward, 1993). Therefore, leaders must help members understand how attention to group interactions directly relate to task purpose and goals.

Balance is best achieved through attention to warm-up, action, and closure. We have chosen the bell-shaped curve to visually depict a group over time (see Figure P2.1).

The figure reflects Jacob Moreno's emphasis on phases or stages in psychodrama groups (Blatner, 1988). The curve identifies a group's warm-up, action, and closure phases. The thin line represents content, and the heavier supporting line represents process. The position of the two lines represents our view that process influences content. In other words, how the group is facilitated greatly determines what the group accomplishes. When balance has been achieved, the process line supports the content line smoothly and consistently through the progression of the three phases. Thus, warm-up, action, and closure represent the ebb and flow of group work. This visualization helps leaders and members see what a successful group experience might look like.

Within this model are sets of questions that address both content and process issues through the progression of warm-up, action, and closure. As future chapters will show, these questions can be answered by using multiple and creative strategies that fit the need of leaders, members, and the purpose of the group. Our goal is not to be prescriptive and to provide a recipe of techniques; rather, we provide examples and stories about how to bring the model to life in task groups. By considering task groups in business, health care, education, legislative, volunteer, and community settings, we illustrate how you can use the concepts in our model to guide your work as a leader and to enhance the likelihood that your task groups will be both productive and enjoyable.

As you will recall, Chapter 1 began with a quotation from Heider emphasizing the importance of being aware of process rather than gather-

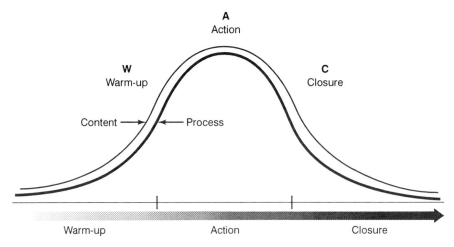

FIGURE P2.1
Balanced process and content in task groups

ing a bag of techniques or gimmicks. Once you are clear about the major concepts to consider when planning and implementing a group, your own ideas for strategies will evolve, and you will become confident, effective, and spontaneous.

In the following chapters, we continue to use the six scenarios introduced in Chapter 1. To bring warm-up, action, and closure into even sharper focus and to enliven the range of concepts presented, we draw on the stories that our distinguished contributors have written especially for this book. We invited them to prepare presentations from their particular settings, asking them, in a very personal way, to relate stories about the role of task groups in these settings and in particular the presence (or absence) of warm-up, action, and closure. We invite you now to meet our friends and their stories.

Profile of Contributors

AL ALCAZAR directs the Community Action Program at Loyola University (LUCAP) in New Orleans, Louisiana. His group stories come from three different settings:

1. The Smoky Mountain Group outside Manila in the Philippines lives in a place very different from the beautiful mountain range in North Carolina. These Smoky Mountains are piles of trash that are some-

times more than 400 feet high. Around these mountains live nearly 20,000 families who survive on what they can find to eat and sell from the "fresh" trash unloaded every day by city trucks.

2. Bridging the Gap (BTG) is primarily a student organization at Loyola University in New Orleans that comes together to learn practical skills for dealing with prejudice and racism in the university setting.

3. The Jeremiah Group is a multifaith and multirace grassroots organization in New Orleans that gathers the talents, energies, and commitments of diverse religious congregations in hopes "of seeking the welfare of the city."

MARY CATHCART is a state senator in Maine. Her group stories are drawn from the legislative committees that she co-chairs and serves on in the Maine State Legislature.

ISSY CROSS is the director of counseling and **MARY FRENNING** is a teacher at Belfast Area High School in Belfast, Maine. Their stories center on the Sophomore Awareness Program, an annual springtime event at their school for nearly 10 years.

ALICE CRYER-SUMLER is a school-to-career specialist in the St. Charles Parish Public Schools in Luling, Louisiana. Her group experiences are varied and include being a member of an administrative team, chairing several committees, and facilitating small groups for children. She has written about a children's group in a school setting. In general, task groups focus on adult situations, but Alice shows that a children's group can also effectively employ warm-up, action, and closure.

COURTLAND LEE is dean and professor of counselor education at Hunter College in New York City and was the 1997–1998 president of the American Counseling Association (ACA). His contribution focuses on the Multicultural Diversity Leadership Summit held in Indianapolis, Indiana, in August 1997. The goal of the summit was to bring the leaders of the ACA stakeholders groups together to develop a comprehensive multicultural/ diversity agenda for the association.

JOHN PHILLIPS is a retired professor of health sciences at the State University of New York—Brockport. His writing focuses on the work of the Finger Lakes Health Systems Agency, which covers a nine-county region in upstate New York. John has been the voluntary president of the agency's executive board. The agency makes certificate of need recommendations to the state for local health care providers. Certificate of need requires providers to undergo a public review process for any significant changes in the delivery of health services.

DON REICHARD became president of Johnston Community College in North Carolina in January 1999. Previously he was president of James Sprunt Community College (JSCC). JSCC is one of a number of colleges practicing community-based programming (C-BP), in which the college facilitates the creation of broad coalitions to address major community issues. At JSCC Don formed a broad community coalition to create the countywide leadership training center he writes about in this book.

LARRY STOKES is the chief executive officer of a small business in New Orleans, Louisiana, and has spent his business career in advertising and software development. His stories are drawn from task group meetings that occurred in three businesses among people whose collaborative skills were already sharply honed and exercised daily.

Chapter 2 takes a close look at warm-up and how planning and preparation can help leaders of task groups achieve their goals.

CHAPTER TWO

An Illustration of the Model for Task Groups in Action: The Warm-up Phase

In the warm-up phase there are three questions to guide leader behavior. Two are process questions: "Who am I?" "Who am I with you?" The third is a content question: "What do we have to do?" If leaders address these questions early in the life of the group, they attend to both the process and content issues necessary for the group as a whole to begin a productive journey.

This phase connects with a number of the assumptions stated in chapter 1. For example, by addressing "Who am I?" and "Who am I with you?" the leader helps a group of individuals learn about one another and to become oriented to the names, faces, beliefs, attitudes, styles, and perspectives that each brings to the group. Several outcomes may be expected from this approach, including the development of cooperation, the understanding and appreciation of differences, and the active participation of members. If both process and content are addressed in the warm-up phase, the process and content lines will resemble the movement up the left side of the curve as seen in Figure P2.1. In many groups, however, distortions can occur. As Figure 2.1 shows, there is often a frenetic focus on productivity.

Notice how the group plunges into the work, the task, the agenda with no attention to process. The content line looms, and the process line stays relatively flat. The visualization in Figure 2.1 could be verbalized as "Let's get going; we have lots to do and not much time, so turn to the first item on the agenda."

Richard may have fallen into this trap. In his meeting multiple perspectives and opinions were operating. However, he moved immediately into content and only later recognized that he needed to address the different perspectives in the room. Consider, too, the explosion in Jane's sce-

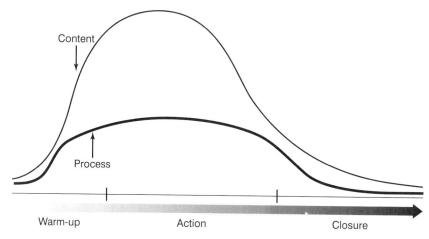

FIGURE 2.1
Richard's dilemma: There are as many opinions and perspectives in this group as there are members.

nario. Did she take the necessary time to put differences on the table and help members get acquainted, clarify expectations, and express their needs before moving into budget discussions? The urgency of tackling the budget seems to have taken precedence over building a climate for addressing potentially emotional issues. Task leaders may not often realize that intentional and thoughtful coalition building actually contributes to successful outcomes.

If an overriding focus on content is problematic, an overemphasis on process can also create problems for the task group leader. Figure 2.2 is another view of a poor warm-up phase. Here the leader incorporates an icebreaker exercise to help members learn about each other. Unfortunately, the effort is not connected to the purpose of the group in a way that is meaningful, convincing, and appropriate for members. The illustration notes a strong process line followed by a strong content line, but the lines are unrelated. Any warm-up activity will fail when it is not clearly linked to the goals of the group and when there is no time to reflect on one's participation in the group activities (Kees & Jacobs, 1990).

Paul's situation with his landscape business employees immediately comes to mind. If Paul convenes a meeting of his employees and begins with a personal "get-to-know-you" activity, he is likely to quickly disengage his workers. Some have already stated their misgivings about touchy-feely time. Recalling Maria's scenario, we can guess that she is also in a challenging spot. She recognizes that differences in verbal expression exist in her group, and she wants to make sure that everyone feels welcome to contribute to the group effort. While she can be applauded for wanting to attend to process issues, her challenge is to create an activity

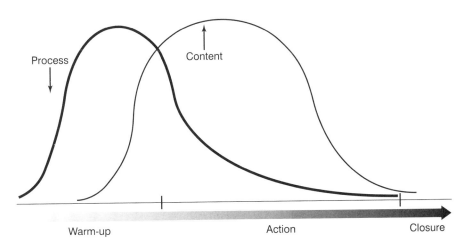

FIGURE 2.2
Paul's challenge: Getting to know one another without creating a touchy-feely time.

that will be relevant to members as they prepare to address the goals of the recreation committee. In her quest to "get along," she might overlook or suppress the content. Figure 2.3 shows how the process and content lines in such a scenario are out of balance. To avoid this trap, Maria must realize that content has an important role to play, and she must be particularly vigilant about connecting her process activities to content to correct this visual distortion.

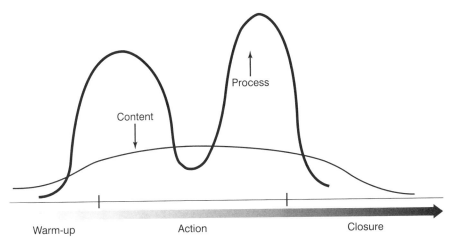

FIGURE 2.3
Maria's quandary: We need to get along first; then we can agree on a location for this playground.

Without a clear connection to purpose or time to reflect on the meaning of ice breakers and other process activities, group leaders and members may find themselves caught in a situation like Figure 2.3's. For example, imagine that Maria says, "Okay, why don't we go around the room and tell something about ourselves. Nancy, you go first." Unless she is thinking conceptually about the link between getting acquainted and the selection of a site for the new community playground, she is likely to end the activity by saying, "Well, now that we have done that, let's move on to planning this playground." How do you think members will respond? Likely, they will feel frustrated, perhaps angry, for what seems to be a waste of time. Their view of process will be tainted by this meaningless experience, and in future groups they may be hesitant or even unwilling to engage in any effort designed to orient people to one another. We have found, however, that most members do respond favorably to an activity that has a clear and relevant connection to the group's purpose and to their present and future participation as contributing members of the group.

Let's return to Richard, Jane, Paul, and Maria to illustrate some strategies that may correct the distortions in Figures 2.2 and 2.3. In all instances the leaders know that their group members will work together for a period of time on important issues. Thus, they should link the importance of getting acquainted and learning about member resources with accomplishing the goals of their group.

For example, imagine that Richard asks his teachers to mention one thing that excites them about teaching English and one challenge they face with their job. He quickly discovers both divergent and convergent viewpoints that can be used in the service of the group. At least now he has some idea of what each person values.

Jane already knows that budget discussions can be stressful because there are so many needs and so few resources. Imagine that she asks her members to introduce themselves and indicate their funding priorities. She also asks members to identify any other issues they believe the group needs to know to make thoughtful budget decisions.

Paul must orient his employees to each other in a way that does not seem touchy-feely. Rephrasing Richard's question might work here: "Since business has really picked up and we are in high demand, I want us to use all the ideas each of you brings so this business will continue to grow and succeed. What do you really like about working in this job? What is your idea for making our landscaping business thrive?"

Maria can maximize the success of her first meeting by using a round to invite members to speak about why the playground is important to them and why they chose to be on this committee. Often in community volunteer groups, some members speak tentatively, while others are eager to share ideas and make points. Sometimes this verbal imbalance is a function of members' work roles. Some may have professional positions outside the group (perhaps professor, doctor, administrator); others may work in less visible or prestigious jobs (school janitor, homemaker, cashier). By setting up a round in which each person gets to speak and form a place in the group, Maria can evaluate the various verbal styles and levels of confidence. She can then relate that information back to the group, saying, "The task of locating land and then building this playground requires everyone's input. Each person has something to contribute. To include all ideas, I may need to stop the action from time to time to make sure that we are hearing from everybody."

It is clear, then, that the tone set during the warm-up phase has a great influence on what goes on as the task group progresses. In most groups members either verbally or quietly ask themselves, "Am I in the group or out of the group?" Members can be physically present and still be absent. The challenge for leaders is to begin shaping a culture that hooks members into believing that this group experience will be productive and satisfying. As Donigian and Malnati (1997) have observed, "culture building also reflects increasing acceptance regarding what is talked about (content) and how it is talked about (process) as well as perceived safety of members" (p. 38).

We often begin our task groups with a brief statement about the group's purpose and the fact that we will be working together for a period of time to achieve our goals. We acknowledge the many potential resources that each member brings and observe that we can maximize our chances for success by learning who we are as individuals and what resources we bring that can help us complete the task and assist others in the group. We note that diversity can be a real asset and that we need to begin understanding who we are and how we might effectively work together using our differences and similarities. A direct statement about our belief that coalition building strengthens our chances for success helps make that important link between the content (purpose) and the process (how group members interrelate). This warm-up phase is comparable to the various stages described in group work literature: the orientation stage (Donigian & Malnati, 1997; Tuckman & Jensen, 1977), the forming stage (Corey & Corey, 1997), and the security stage (Trotzer, 1989). It involves designing a climate in which members feel safe to be themselves. Helping people get acquainted and providing clarity about purpose contribute to this sense of safety and strengthen the foundation for mutual trust (Donigian & Malnati, 1997).

Warm-up Themes

Seven themes have emerged from our discussion about warm-up:

1. Getting acquainted
2. Understanding the purpose of the group

3. Linking process information to the group's purpose
4. Recognizing why member participation is important to the group's work
5. Recognizing why attention to diversity is important to the group's work
6. Creating guidelines for behavior in the group
7. Recognizing individual resources and strengths in the group

Let's turn our attention to how our contributors reflect on these themes in their own task groups.

Getting Acquainted

Our contributors vary in how they address this theme in their groups. Issy Cross and Mary Frenning describe their Sophomore Awareness Program:

> Sophomore Awareness has been an annual springtime event at Belfast Area High School for close to a decade. For three days sophomores are taken off campus to participate in a program that brings a whole class together to listen to and discuss presentations related to contemporary social issues, ethical dilemmas, and questions of individual and group personal concern. An added benefit of the experience is the evolution of a sense of class unity at the end of the three days.
>
> The initial small group session (the time when all groups meet for the first time), is devoted largely to a successful warm-up. This is the time for participants to establish a group comfort level. Ice breaker and getting-to-know-you activities are used at this stage. Lots of questions and concerns are anticipated and should be addressed.

Don Reichard reflects on several early coalition meetings at James Sprunt Community College:

> Participants used a name and expectations exercise. They were asked to state their name, where they live, their organization affiliation, and what they expected to happen in the coalition work. In subsequent groups participants were given time for introductions and were welcomed by the leader. The leader's introduction of the expected outcomes for the first meeting was warm and upbeat and engendered excitement in the group.

Larry Stokes's approach is similar to Don's:

In all task settings, the warm-up includes the convening of the group and a determination of who each member is and what each member's task will be.

State senator Mary Cathcart observes a different style:

The only thing we do by way of introductions is ask, "Who are you?" "What do you do?" (Most people have an occupation besides the legislature or are retired from one.) We simply are not given time for team-building activities. Even if there was time, some members might refuse to participate. If you began some of these get-acquainted activities, they might walk out of the room, saying, "This is not what we are here to do."

Courtland Lee describes a particular activity designed to help his ACA multicultural summit group members become acquainted with each other:

The summit began with an activity that gave participants the opportunity to introduce themselves in a personal as opposed to professional manner. This exercise is based on the Hangi welcome ceremony of the Maori people of New Zealand. The Maori are the indigenous people of New Zealand, who for generations have lived a group-oriented life closely linked to nature. As part of the activity, participants introduced themselves to the group in the following manner:

My mountain(s)_____

My river(s)_____

My tribe(s)_____

I am_____

Participants were encouraged to talk about their river and mountain of origin, their family of origin, and their given name. This activity allowed group members to reflect on their relationship to nature and their links to family. It also took the focus away from leadership positions and titles. I told them that in the Maori tradition a sharing such as this resulted in the formation of a Marae—a communal gathering place. Among the Maori people, it is in the Marae that important group decisions are made. I expected that, in the spirit of the Maori, this group of ACA leaders would form a Marae.

From a process perspective, this activity had a profound effect on the summit participants. They commented that sharing personal, nonprofessional information about themselves was very freeing. They felt a new closeness to other members of the group. Several leaders commented that, in listening to particular group members talk about their rivers and mountains, chords of familiarity were struck. In addition, they all indicated that they wanted to use the activity as part of team-building activities with their own entities.

Courtland Lee's approach is similar Al Alcazar's approach with the Smoky Mountain Group:

> The groups with which I have been involved all start with a deliberate plan to transgress the oppressor's (racist, sexist, classist, heterosexist, specialist, etc.) style of educating and group leading (herding?). Close to the way bell hooks (1994) described it, transgression meant, on the one hand, an active and persistent rejection of the oppressor's prescribed reality, a dislodging of this reality from the core of our being and, on the other, a passionate reclaiming of our dignity as human beings—a task that includes solidarity with other living creatures.

> For the women in the Smoky Mountain, the warm-up phase of our gathering started as soon as they left their homes on their way to our meetings, when they began to silently recite the group mantra: "For so long, because I am poor, I have been treated like I am already dead; but I know now that my poverty is a historical situation and the result of a political decision, not the will of God; I am a child of God and I will use sacred anger in my heart to change my situation by working together with my neighbors to seek justice for myself, for my children, and for my community." This is followed by each group member's answer to the questions "What do you think your parents were thinking when they gave you your name?" "What situations have you been in that made you feel nameless?"

> Each group member walks through the neighborhood and finds the newest "discard" (families who have been evicted or prostitutes who now have children or are too old for the job). Stories of turning a discard into a neighbor also become part of the warm-up phase, and their plights keep the purpose of our group alive and urgent.

> With people living in extreme poverty, situations that seem ordinary to middle-class folks are almost always so urgent that their identities and relatedness in the group are at times neglected. One of the crucial tasks for the leader was to make sure this did not happen; otherwise, we fell into "activism among strangers" instead of "activism among neighbors."

A range of task and other groups are regularly organized in schools. Alice Cryer-Sumler considers her work with middle school children's groups:

> To effectively meet the many needs of middle school students, it was crucial for me to design a structured plan for working with students. On an average, I ran four groups each day with students in fifth through eighth grade, with fifth and sixth graders grouped together and seventh and eighth graders grouped together. This arrangement assisted somewhat with the varying levels of maturity.
>
> Each day before the first group of students arrived, I arranged the room in a circular format with stuffed animals on each chair. The students were encouraged to hold the animals during the group process if they chose to do so or simply place them on another chair. Most students wanted to hold a stuffed animal during our group time, which was approximately 45 minutes long. They told me the stuffed animals made them feel comfortable as they participated in the discussion groups.
>
> I waited at the door to greet students as they entered the room. When they entered, they said, "Good morning" "Good afternoon" to their fellow group members. After they settled in with their stuffed animals, I welcomed everyone to the group for that day and asked everyone to introduce him or herself to make new members feel comfortable.
>
> All our groups began with an ice breaker initiated by a student or me. Typically, I asked the students to check in using a weather descriptor, a football or a basketball play, or a line from a song as a gauge to let group members know where they were for that day. Sometimes a student said, "I feel like a bright sunny day because I made a B on my test." But another might say, "I feel like a storm is coming because I know my father is still using heroin and he will be arrested soon." This check-in process was a powerful strategy for involving middle school students in the warm-up phase of the group.

Learning Points.   From our contributors we have learned that

1. Sharing some personal information can be relevant to the functioning of a task group.
2. In some task settings personal sharing is devalued and considered irrelevant to the group's purpose.
3. Members appreciate a leader's warm, genuinely welcoming style.

4. Getting acquainted can help establish a group norm of collaboration.
5. Warm-up can build group cohesiveness.
6. Creative warm-up activities are needed to fit the needs of different populations and settings.

Understanding the Purpose of the Group

While getting acquainted taps the process side of group work, understanding the purpose taps the content side. Courtland Lee tells us:

> I presented the goal, general objectives, and expected outcome for the summit. The goal was to develop a comprehensive and coordinated 21st-century multicultural/diversity agenda for the American Counseling Association. The general objectives were to (1) assess ACA's progress in advancing multiculturalism and diversity and (2) chart a strategic course for further action to ensure that ACA is a truly multicultural association. The expected outcome was to develop a multicultural/diversity agenda complete with a statement of principles, leadership goals, and action strategies.
>
> I reviewed with summit participants a series of both internal and external challenges and opportunities facing the counseling profession. These served as the rationale for developing a strategic plan for addressing issues of multiculturalism and diversity.

Al Alcazar notes the three interrelated purposes of the Smoky Mountain Group:

> Our purposes were to (1) demand decent housing, (2) keep the bulldozers from destroying members' cardboard box homes, and (3) tell the truth about the exploitation of women in the hospitality and entertainment industry.

Don Reichard says:

> At the first meeting, members learned about community-based programming (C-BP) and how the coalition would be performing the most important task in the model (development of a plan of action) and how long their work would last (three two-hour meetings).
>
> Between the first and second coalition meetings, the leaders analyzed the results of the small group work. Enclosed with the announcement of the second meeting were a draft of a mission

statement, a draft set of guiding principles, and a suggestion for the development of four internal components for the institute: program, marketing/public relations, resource development, and management/operations. For each component there was a list of the elements, thoughts, suggestions, or ideas that had emerged in the five breakout sessions during the first coalition meeting.

All were taken from the suggestions at the first meeting. In other words, we were using the products of the coalition, not injecting outside expertise that could give the coalition the feeling that its work was not valuable. Next, a general outline of the agenda was presented in the cover letter. Members were asked to be prepared when they arrived to indicate which component they wanted to work on in the planned subgroup sessions.

The invitation was also mailed to potential members who were unable to attend the first meeting. They were welcomed to the coalition, asked to review all material, and encouraged to call a leader if they had questions. As a result, several new members came to the second coalition meeting.

At the third meeting, the mission and guiding principles were reviewed again, which helped educate new members and warmed up all members for their work at this last meeting.

The leaders and the steering committee did an excellent job of designing activities to clarify the purpose of the coalition. The introduction by a coalition member was intended to give meaning and importance to the planned work of the coalition. (It did.) The brief reports on the previous accomplishments of the coalition gave legitimacy to why leadership was the issue at hand and why it was critical to the future success of Duplin County.

Mary Cathcart describes how a legislative group addresses purpose:

In addition to the members, each committee is assigned a staff analyst, who does most of the research needed to inform the legislators, and a committee clerk, who is responsible for scheduling hearings, work sessions, presentations, and so on.

With the committee I chair, at our opening session we held a little orientation especially for new members. The analyst talked about her role and how an analyst can be helpful in doing research on legislation.

In the Sophomore Awareness Program Issy Cross and Mary Frenning invite their students to create the purpose:

Sophomores are asked to complete a questionnaire and to prioritize the topics of greatest interest and concern to them. The design of the three-day program is based largely on the questionnaire results. The committee then develops plans for an overall theme and schedules the topics to be presented. Each topic or issue is evaluated in terms of potential sensitivity, and the need to address these topics is delicately balanced with climate, characteristics, and unique community distinctions. Communication with the superintendent, principal, teachers, and sophomore parents is maintained throughout the planning stages.

The speakers and their placement in the program are then determined within the three-day time frame. The next task is to confirm the availability of the presenters. (The 1999 program included an ethical decision-making educator; a diversity and tolerance panel; a lawyer knowledgeable about teenage parenting responsibilities; a suicide and grief panel; a case worker and two state prisoners speaking about crime prevention; several short, theme-based interactive theater performances; a monologue by a professional actress addressing dating violence; and a hospital emergency room nurse's drinking and driving presentation).

Learning Points.   We have gleaned the following from our contributors:

1. Clarity of purpose and timelines increase productivity.
2. Providing brief updates on the group's progress energizes members.
3. Referring back to the importance of the purpose gives meaning and value to the work of the task group.
4. Clearly defined purposes are like an effective rudder on a ship, controlling the group's direction.

Linking Process Information to the Group's Purpose

One of the points in our model for task groups is the need to make a connection between process and content. Mary Cathcart has mentioned that, in a legislative group, if someone introduces process activities in the form of getting acquainted or team building, legislators may not see any reason for them and decline to engage or simply leave. Her observation captures the response of many people in task groups, who may not see why the group should address process issues. Leaders have an obligation to provide meaning and relevance, especially to any activities related to personal relationships in task settings. Let's look at how some of our contributors made connections between process and content.

Don Reichard recalls his group's introductions phase:

> Members became aware that the coalition represented a diverse group with representatives from all across the county. This recognition of diversity excited the group, giving it a sense that something new, different, and important was going to happen.

It is clear, then, that the convenors were attempting to link the purpose to why it was important to learn about one another, and members recognized that link. Similarly, in subsequent meetings, new members were given a chance to introduce themselves and were made to feel part of the group. The leaders spent a few minutes and gave members an opportunity to clarify questions. The group was then ready to move ahead.

Al Alcazar reminds us that in his groups it was important to nurture relationships and to help members recognize that learning "Who am I with you?" is directly related to the purpose of the group:

> "Who am I?" and "What do we have to do?" will not keep the group together (warm) without the bridging and bonding power of "Who am I with you?" The power generated by this question literally saved our lives in the detention center during one long horrifying night of interrogation, when a soldier used a loaded 45-caliber pistol to trace question marks on our foreheads along with other terrifying questioning techniques. Only confidence that the other members of the group would see to our welfare kept us from breaking psychologically.

This brings to light, in a dramatic way, how knowledge of one another and the relationships among members can become a powerful force in not only supporting the group's purpose but taking care of one another.

Learning Points.   We have learned that

1. Issues and products can actually evolve from relationships made in the task group.
2. In groups with a social justice mission, it is crucial that the focus on culture-building activities be given the same weight as the focus on content.
3. Helping members feel part of the group can actually contribute to member commitment to work on the task at hand.
4. In some groups a climate of safety can help the group maintain itself.

Recognizing Why Member Participation
Is Important to the Group's Work

Larry Stokes reflects on this theme:

> As a leader in the business, I am often the leader of a smaller
> group. I have learned that to be a leader means to allow the mem-
> bers to determine the strategies and paths taken to accomplish the
> goals of the group. I must allow the success to happen and the
> goals to be accomplished. Each member is an ingredient of a
> group that is greater than the sum of its parts.

> Throughout the day many teams convene to perform tasks and
> solve problems. In our work setting, ideas do not come from one
> person. They more often come from a collaboration among several
> individuals to solve problems and accomplish tasks that are part
> of our business. There is much action in a day in a small business
> setting. Companies must be responsive to their customers' needs,
> which means having a willing and eager team of experts to
> respond and deliver the services. The way to success for me has
> been to surround myself with successful people. This means
> becoming part of a team as the leader or as a member, often lead-
> ing by following because of the expertise of the team's member-
> ship. What happens to create a group or team? In my experience,
> it is the desire to assist because of the common goal, which is con-
> tinued success.

Courtland Lee has a similar perspective on members as resources:

> Participants were invited to share what their respective entities
> were doing to advance multiculturalism and diversity in counsel-
> ing. This discussion provided baseline information for the devel-
> opment of a comprehensive strategic agenda for the entire associa-
> tion.

Issy Cross and Mary Frenning focus on member participation:

> Critical to the Sophomore Awareness Program is the establish-
> ment of small-group breakout sessions to follow each large-group
> topic presentation. The number in each of these groups is limited
> to 8 to 12 students to allow more time for individual reflection
> and response.

Alice Cryer-Sumler actively encourages participation:

I remind the students that they need to participate in the process to really enjoy the benefits of group work.

In Don Reichard's group, members were welcomed and recognized for their contributions.

In the opening meeting members were told that there were no adult leadership programs in the county but more than 100 in the state (stressing the need for their involvement). The needs survey showed a wide desire for leadership training, and the focus of the Gulf Coast program was on grassroots citizenship training. In addition, a cover letter was sent to all members before the third meeting: "What a pleasure it is to share the results of the excellent work you coalition members completed at the second meeting on Monday, June 23. When this project is actually up and running, complete with a wide range of leadership education and training activities, the details of the level of work in which we are presently engaged may not seem very important or exciting. However, because of the time and care and effort that the coalition is now expending in this planning and design stage, a real foundation is being creatively laid on which a wide range of useful programs for our county can be successfully developed. So a huge bravo to all concerned for your fine efforts to date."

Again, attention was being given to the caring of the group by enhancing its self-concept. It was hoped that such attention would encourage all members to attend the coalition meeting.

From his health care setting, John Phillips recalls:

The leader must remain certain that everyone is heard from (even by a "What do you think?" aimed at members less inclined to speak out but whose opinion may be critical). It is my sense that these leader behaviors help prevent domination of opinions and provide a more balanced approach to content.

It is also my experience that there must be periodic celebrations of accomplishments in some form of social get-togethers. I am convinced that celebrations and humor greatly help in maintaining a satisfying group experience.

Al Alcazar provides us a conceptual framework for understanding the difference between the leader as the person running the show versus an energizing and empowering membership:

The women in the Smoky Mountains would often say to me: "What can we really do? We are just a bunch of scavengers." Or in other situations, they would say, "We can't do that. Have you forgotten that shyness [*docility* is probably the better word] is our national trait?"

The Brazilian educator and organizer Paulo Freire (1970) points out that "docility is the fruit of an historical and sociological situation, not an essential characteristic of a people's behavior" (p. 48). This historical-sociological situation was effectively maintained by what Freire calls the banking approach to education, in which the oppressor deposits or prescribes the knowledge in the docile and passive receptacles in the minds of the oppressed. In this maintenance approach to education,

1. the teacher teaches and the students are taught;
2. the teacher knows everything and the students know nothing;
3. the teacher thinks and the students are thought about;
4. the teachers talk and the students listen meekly;
5. the teacher disciplines and the students are disciplined;
6. the teacher chooses and enforces his choice and the students comply;
7. the teacher acts and the student follows;
8. the teacher chooses the program content and the students who were not consulted adapt to it;
9. the teacher confuses the authority of knowledge with his own professional authority, which he sets in opposition to the freedom of the students;
10. the teacher is the subject of the learning process, while the students are mere objects. (p. 59)

I quote Freire at length here because the warm-up, action, and closure model is not only consistent with Freire's concept of a dialogical leader but also an effective antidote to the banking approach to education and its counterparts in group work.

Learning Points.   The learning points for active member participation are

1. Members are the group's best resource.
2. Participation of all is needed to ensure that all talents are brought to the goals of the task group.
3. Hearing from all participants gives leaders baseline data about how all players view the task group goals.
4. When leaders recognize and engage members, the members feel more invested in the group's purpose and objectives.

5. Celebrations of accomplishments can acknowledge and reinforce member contributions.

6. Engaging members helps them move from positions of docility and acquiescence to positions of inclusion, empowerment, and contribution.

Recognizing Why Attention to Diversity Is Important to the Group's Work

Courtland Lee observes:

> Participants were also asked to identify and discuss the current paradigms that form the basis of multicultural counseling theory, practice, and research. Through discussion it became clear that people came to the meeting with a number of personal and professional agendas as well as many preconceived notions. Most of these agendas and notions were put on the table at this point and provided an important context for participants' deliberations over the course of the summit. They also provided an important creative tension and energy that stimulated the work of the group.

> After discussion participants were invited to share what their respective entities were doing to advance multiculturalism and diversity in counseling. These data provided baseline information for the development of a comprehensive strategic agenda for the entire association.

Issy Cross and Mary Frenning see the importance of attending to diversity for both the facilitators and members of the Sophomore Awareness Groups:

> Recruitment and training of co-facilitators to lead these groups is a very important task considering that facilitators play such a crucial role in the success of the program and its value to students. When recruiting adult co-facilitators, several factors are considered: experience with adolescents, diversity (gender, professional background, age), flexibility and adaptability, as well as availability for a three-day commitment (in addition to a separate three-hour training session a week before the program).

> When assigning students to small groups, we consider gender balance, diversity, separation of cliques, and temperament. Once student groups are established, sophomore peer leaders are paired

and assigned to each group. Their task, for which they have earlier in the year received extensive training, involves modeling group behavior, supporting the inclusion of all members in the discussion process, and assisting the adult co-facilitators. The co-facilitators are then paired using criteria similar to those used in assigning students: diversity, experience in the group process, and previous service to the program.

Mary Cathcart considered whether the atmosphere in legislative groups was collegial or adversarial:

> We try to make it collegial. Obviously, because of some legislation we have to deal with, there are partisan differences, and it gets really adversarial. For the most part committees work with some decorum and courtesy toward other members. Usually we can disagree without getting angry, although there are partisan differences, and they are basic to the political process.

Larry Stokes offers this account:

> When the members went off to conduct their task, they entered into another collaboration with other parties to achieve those tasks. This is something that happens quite frequently in the work setting. For example, once the information was gathered for the corporation's salary survey, the information was dictated and given to two different people to transcribe the dictations. The parts were then merged to form one completed report. The two transcriptionists collaborated to get the report out in a timely manner.

Learning Points.   Learning points include

1. Discovering various viewpoints and needs can energize group members.
2. By addressing differences up front, leaders and members can design mechanisms to manage the expression of those differences.
3. Attending to differences and similarities uncovers individual strengths and abilities that can be used to reach the goals of the task group.
4. The presence of different views can stimulate what Palmer refers to as creative conflict (1987) and provide the group with vitality.
5. Placing differences on the table minimizes the presence of hidden agendas.

6. Diversity energizes the development of content (i.e., what will be addressed) and process (i.e., how it will be addressed).

Creating Guidelines for Behavior in the Group

Don Reichard says:

> I cannot underscore too much the importance of ground rules. Time and time again, the leaders were able to keep the discussions in the general and subgroup meetings moving along productively by referring back to the ground rules (which were displayed for all to see at every meeting). The rules on full participation, listening to others, capturing words as stated on the flip chart, and respect for the process were used most often to avoid dominance by a few members and to resolve conflicts.

Issy Cross and Mary Frenning have guidelines for promoting the content and process of their groups:

> Participants should establish and accept group rules and operating procedures. Among the essential rules are confidentiality and no put-downs. If these rules do not come from the group, the facilitator may introduce them for discussion. Additional rules to fit individual group needs should be developed, such as permission to pass and use of I-statements.

Alice Cryer-Sumler recalls:

> Before each group session began, group members reviewed the group rules on a poster.

Mary Cathcart reflects on legislative groups:

> Each committee passes its own rules having to do with when you can speak, eating and drinking in hearings, and other details. We vote on the rules, and they are adopted and passed on to the presiding officers of the House and Senate.
>
> There is not much discussion about the rules. They follow a fairly standard model used by most committees. There may be slight variations, such as having food at work sessions when there is no time for lunch.

Don Reichard discusses the presentation of ground rules in his coalition group:

> Present and review the ground rules. Ask members if they understand and support ground rules. This dialogue builds group norms.
>
> *Ground Rules*
> 1. Thou shalt participate fully.
> 2. Thou shalt actually listen to what others say.
> 3. Thou shalt accept what others say as valid.
> 4. Thou shalt share responsibility for making these meetings a success.
> 5. Thou shalt not dictate, even if thou art the expert.
> 6. Thou shalt not censor thyself or others during brainstorming.
> 7. Thou shalt encourage fresh ideas, new perspectives, and crazy notions.
> 8. Thou shalt ensure that thy words are captured on the flip charts.
> 9. Thou shalt respect the process.
> 10. Thou shalt realize that this is the beginning and that we must follow through.

Learning Points.   Two important points emerge from our contributors' reflections:

1. Referring back to ground rules can keep the group on task and minimize disruptive conversation.
2. Rules build norms and standards of conduct that contribute to the development of a group culture.

Recognizing Individual Resources and Strengths in the Group

Larry Stokes shows how attention to member resources and strengths occurs in his work setting:

> As the life plan team begins to enter the conference room, we start discussing the case to determine how we will develop a plan. To begin, I, as the team leader, inform team members how they came

to be chosen for this task. Since this case involves a child who has been exposed to lead and has experienced cognitive deficits, our nurse specialist has been included to assist with the medical aspects of the case. Another member, whose special interest is in child development and education, has been chosen to assist. A veteran member with 30 years' experience in the field of rehabilitation counseling has been chosen to direct the development of the plan for therapeutic modalities, equipment, services, and recreation and leisure activities. He will also be able to determine the frequency and duration of each service and type of equipment so that the associated costs can be reviewed. Charlene, because of her pleasant demeanor and tenacious research ability, has been chosen to survey the costs associated with this life care plan.

After informing members of the assignment, they eagerly volunteer for the very tasks that they have been chosen for. This is no coincidence. My job, as the team leader, is to identify the talents and interests of the team members to enlist their participation in the team and enable them to achieve the goals of the assignment. We meet for about an hour, discussing tasks and assignments, brainstorming the strategy. Then we depart but not before we schedule a follow-up meeting one week from today to determine our progress.

The leader does not assign tasks in most situations. The leader allows the members to choose their tasks based on their strengths and abilities. This choice allows for cooperation and collaboration, building the group through a discovery of their similarities and differences. The process and content are supported by the group system as well as by each member as a subsystem.

The individual strengths and interests are celebrated because one person cannot be an expert in all areas. Each one's strength comes together to build the team that accomplishes the goal. Each develops and maintains mutual respect through this cooperation, collaboration, and recognition of strengths.

Learning Points.   Learning points include

1. Identifying individual member talents and harnessing those talents collectively can strengthen the work of a task group.

2. Celebrating individual talents and strengths builds self-confidence and self-esteem among task group members.

3. Mutual respect is enhanced through encouraging cooperation and collaboration.

Summary of Themes and Contributors' Reflections

In reviewing the themes and comments, we note several points. Task group members may hesitate to employ getting-acquainted activities because of their negative connotations. Mary Cathcart's statement about legislative groups comes to mind. It seems that many people view such activities as touchy-feely, intrusive, irrelevant, and valueless. However, Al Alcazar, Courtland Lee, Larry Stokes, Alice Cryer-Sumler, Don Reichard, Issy Cross, and Mary Frenning observed that a warm, welcoming, genuinely caring demeanor is relevant to task groups. They believe that time spent getting acquainted can be strategically linked to the work of the group. Issy and Mary's description of the Sophomore Awareness Program captures the essence of cooperation and collaboration, which they recognize as their key to success. As Al notes, without some attention to connections among members, task groups will complete their goals among strangers instead of neighbors. Thus, an important learning point is that some orientation to people is needed. Leaders need to define and present this orientation using activities, exercises, or experiences that complement the population and goals of the group. To ignore relationships is to miss a critical aspect of the group's functioning.

A number of our contributors believe that getting to know one another helps members identify the strengths and resources that each member brings to the group endeavor. Members' views about the task at hand, their potential contributions, and the differences in working styles are just a few of the factors that can be addressed when leaders help members get to know one another.

Reflecting on the warm-up phase in his coalition, Don Reichard observes:

> First, the more preplanning using the warm-up concepts, the better. Our members were not the typical 30 to 40 community leaders that too often belong to every local partnership. About half of the group of more than 60 people were active local leaders. The other half were individuals with little formal leadership experience who saw the coalition as an opportunity to engage in something new and important. In fact, more than half of the participants in the first citizen leadership program came from this part of the coalition. The college wanted the coalition to be a diverse group, which it was. But that meant that the process to produce the product needed to be orchestrated carefully for all phases: warm-up, action, and closure. As it turned out, the preplanning paid off because in most cases all activities went smoothly.
>
> Although the name exercise and expectations exercise went well, in retrospect, I would have spent more time on the "Who am I?"

"Who am I with you?" aspects. I don't think the members gained as much understanding and appreciation for the differences and similarities in their backgrounds as they could have. I would add a movement activity on work preferences and interpersonal styles next time. Also we used the same warm-up technique at each meeting, whereas we could have used a different ice breaker at each session that had a different intent in helping the coalition to build its culture, norms, and trust.

Suggestions for Implementing the Warm-up Phase

Because of the quantity and variety of tools and techniques available to group leaders (e.g., Jacobs, Masson, & Harvill, 1998; Napier & Gerschenfeld, 1983) leaders need only to examine and select strategies that fit their personalities and the needs of their group participants. Here are several ideas that you may find helpful in starting your task groups.

Rounds

Rounds give task group leaders a method for checking in with all members and gathering information. Leaders can attend to "Who am I?" "Who am I with you?" and "What do we have to do?" without resorting to activities that appear too personal, foolish, focused on feelings, or irrelevant. We have noted how Maria might use rounds to identify different verbal styles in her group. Here are several more ideas for using rounds in groups with varying goals and objectives.

In a university public service awards committee meeting, the leader invited members to check in with their name, their university department or unit, and a brief statement about what public service means to them. This exercise served two purposes. First, it provided a structure for members to introduce themselves. In settings such as university committees, often some members are acquainted, but some do not know everyone. No one is willing to say, "I don't know everyone's name." If the leader asks for names, all members learn names and positions. Second, by asking about each member's view of public service, the leader begins to learn where there are convergent and divergent views. If, for example, some members think public service can consist of both paid and nonpaid activities and others strongly believe that public service is only uncompensated work, then there will be clear disagreement when individuals are nominated for awards.

Imagine a research committee of graduate faculty in a college of education. The purpose of this committee is to review the research curriculum at the doctoral level and to make suggestions for creating a balance between offerings that emphasize quantitative research methods and those that focus on qualitative ones. This topic engenders strong viewpoints and feelings. It is also unclear at times what faculty members' definitions of research are. The leader would be well advised to conduct an opening round in which all members state their definition of research. Asking members about their expectations for the work of the committee would add more baseline data for the leader and the members to consider.

Rounds also provide leaders with a quick way to assess the energy in the group. Jacobs et al. (1998) suggest checking in with descriptors such as "here," "not here," "getting here." In any type of task group, this information is invaluable for assessing which members are present to work and which may have distractions that will interfere with their contributions. By knowing where the energy levels are, the leader can plan in advance for how to proceed.

Name Exercise

This is a quick exercise that can begin to connect members and elicit bits of people's stories. Members are asked four questions: "What is your name?" "How did you get your name?" "Do you like your name?" "If not, what name would you choose?" This exercise has the components of a successfully formed activity because it is simple, the questions are short and clear, and it invites a certain sharing of information that is not overly personal or intrusive. In our experience with a number of task groups, this type of activity warms up members and begins to help them learn names and recognize connections with others in the group. Often through discussing the origins of names, members disclose information about their culture and family. This exercise is linked to the recognition that stories can help people connect and learn how they are similar to others and to discover where certain differences, perhaps profound ones, exist (Lappe, 1990).

Richard could have used this activity to break the ice and begin helping newer teachers become acquainted with more experienced ones. This activity can serve as a first step in a series of warm-up rounds. Following the name activity, Richard could move into questions about what excites and challenges teachers. By using both activities, he would model how to balance attention to "Who am I?" "Who am I with you?" and "What do we have to do?"

Microlabs

Microlabs are structured exercises designed to help members get acquainted, develop human relations skills, and relate their personal backgrounds and experiences to the group's content. Microlabs serve as useful strategies for balancing process and content issues in a task group through increasing member-to-member participation while helping participants focus on the learning or work goals for which the group was formed. This particular activity could work well in Maria's group. Remember that she is concerned about making sure that all members participate. Here is an example of what her microlab might look like.

Ask participants to form groups of three or four. Select someone to keep notes and observe timelines. Allow about five minutes for each question.

1. Introduce yourself to each member in your small group and tell why you have joined this committee.
2. Discuss your expectations for being a member on this committee. What expectations do you have for your behavior in the group, the behavior of your community colleagues, and the behavior of your leader? Then reconvene in the larger group and discuss your responses.
3. Back in your small groups, discuss your ideas about locating the new playground. Through consensus select three locations that seem feasible. List the locations on a chart that everyone can see.
4. What are the advantages and disadvantages for each location? List these on the chart. Reconvene in the larger group and discuss your responses.

At this point Maria could work with the entire group by examining the various suggestions and working with members to discover the best options for the committee to pursue. Microlabs are helpful for focusing attention on content while giving all members the opportunity to participate in the discussion. Leaders are invited to design microlabs that fit the needs of their members. Anderson (1981) presents examples of microlabs that can be adapted for groups with multiple and varied goals.

Movement Activities

Activities that give members a chance to move around the room while visually placing themselves in certain positions that correspond to geographics, demographics, time in the organization or work setting, age, and work and leisure preferences are helpful ice breakers. When the leader stops and gives members a chance to comment on their particular positions around the room, they begin to see examples of member-to-member similarities and differences. Here are two variations of this activity.

In *social bingo,* leaders place facts in squares on a piece of paper. Members go around the room to locate others who, for example, have played a musical instrument, traveled abroad, or like to cook. Other facts can be placed in the squares that relate to the particular task group purpose. Members initial the square that fits for them. Leaders will need to take time to discuss the activity so that members recognize its value and potential link to the purpose of the group. For example, Reverend Ellison could use social bingo as a way to help his members take some structured time to get acquainted and to focus on the work of the church. The boxes in social bingo could focus on personal items (e.g., favorite foods, special talents, favorite music) and on topics that correspond to each person's role on the council (e.g., liturgy, education, music). For the members in his group, social bingo would give people a chance to move around, meet new people, and think about the various topics that this particular church needs to address.

Work Preferences and Interpersonal Styles draws on items from the Myers-Briggs Type Indicator (Myers & McCaulley, 1985). These forced-choice items are written in behavioral language and printed on a sheet of paper. For example, members move around the room according to preferences such as "I prefer to talk things out" or "I prefer to think things through"; "I prefer to have the specifics" or "I prefer to work with the big picture"; "I prefer to hear the logical implications of a situation" or "I prefer to learn the impact that a situation has on people before I make a decision"; "I prefer to come to a conclusion quickly" or "I prefer to stay receptive to discussion and keep my options open." Often people will say they fit in the middle, but the movement part invites them to select the one position that is most like them, most of the time, and especially like them for this particular task group setting. As members discuss their positions and what those positions represent to them, everyone begins to glimpse the styles and preferences that will likely become visible and active as the group progresses.

The leaders of our six group scenarios could benefit from this activity. Maria's group comes to mind again as an example. She could note the importance of hearing all views and opinions and suggest that learning members' different styles of relating with others and with information could be helpful.

Group Guidelines

Several activities can be used to help shape healthy norms for the work of a task group. These include examining expectations and developing consensus statements about norms or guidelines for group behavior. Here are some examples.

Examining expectations can assist in developing guidelines related to the purpose of the task group. By asking members to reflect on (a) expectations they have of themselves in the group, (b) what they expect of their fellow colleagues, and (c) what they expect of the leader, valuable data are gathered that can help the leader and members enhance the likelihood of success for the group. Discussions of these expectations uncover discrepancies that can be identified and discussed.

Jane's group immediately comes to mind. In a group that focuses on emotional topics such as budgets, it can be productive to engage members up front in a discussion of their expectations for the committee, how they will interact with one another, and what they want from the leader. By attending to these issues in the beginning, Jane can be alerted to potential problems as well as places where members agree.

We have found it helpful to invite members of task groups to discuss and select *consensus statements* that describe their views about group attendance and participation. After discussing their ideas in small groups, members convene in the larger group to summarize the points that everyone has discussed and to use a "thumbs up" to signal agreement. The leader can present all members with a typed copy of the consensus agreement at the next session. The agreement becomes a contract that can be reviewed throughout the life of the group to check on both process and content issues.

Reverend Ellison might use a consensus statement with the church group. With a clear focus on the topics of attendance and participation, he could refer back to the typed statement when he notices problems in attendance, punctuality, verbal interaction, and so on.

It is crucial for leaders and members to be clear about the content of what can be discussed and how. Human relations issues will be part of the conversation as leaders and members develop guidelines for their work together. Leaders need to make it clear that during the task group they will occasionally offer observations about how the relationship issues in the task group are affecting the work of the group. Two outcomes result from this conversation. If attention to process can be accepted early on as a central part of the group's work, then leaders will not be seen as departing from the purpose of the group when they address here-and-now issues and leaders will not be restricted in addressing the types of relationship issues that are either enhancing or hindering the work of the group.

Use of Clear Language

Leaders can help members be more active participants by encouraging them to use I-statements and begin conversing more freely with other members in the group as well as with the leader. I-statements encourage everyone to speak in the here-and-now in the first person and to direct conversation to others in the group besides the leader. The increase of member bonding is one outcome of direct speech in member-to-member interaction (Donigian & Malnati, 1997).

Leaders can ask members to be aware of language and to provide their feedback and observations in statements that help other members understand the meaning of the statements. "We," "you," "they," and "us" create ambiguity because the listener does not know whether the speaker is speaking for herself or making generalizations. Communication is always clearer and more effective when members use direct, first-person statements.

Final Tips for Leaders During the Warm-up Phase

1. Be prepared. Know your population, their needs, and their special characteristics.
2. Be aware of member concerns.
3. Remember that members are a group's most important resources.
4. Work with the members to create healthy, helpful group guidelines.
5. Help members get acquainted through activities that fit the goal of the group and the characteristics of members.
6. Help members develop empathy for other positions, perspectives, and world views.
7. Discuss individual expectations, expectations of other members, and expectations of the leader.
8. Provide a structure in the form of an agenda to reduce ambiguity and ensure a clear focus.
9. Use skills that involve cutting off, drawing out, holding, and shifting the focus.
10. Provide meaning attribution so that members can learn how what is happening in the task group helps or hinders its goals and purpose.

◆ ◆ ◆

Points to Ponder

1. Explain the significance of having a clear purpose in forming a task group.

2. Explain the critical need for leaders to attend to the warm-up phase each time their task groups meet.

3. Explain what is meant by energizing and empowering task group members and why these elements are important for task group leaders to address.

4. Discuss why leaders must be sensitive and alert to diversity issues in the work of the task group.

5. It is important for leaders to create behavior guidelines for group members. Explain the function such guidelines serve in a task group.

6. Explain why leaders need to maintain a balance between process and content in the warm-up phase and discuss how leaders can facilitate this balance.

◆ ◆ ◆

References

Anderson, W. (1981). Developing appropriate exercises for microlabs. *Journal for Specialists in Group Work, 6,* 211–216.

Blatner, A. (1988). *Acting-in: Practical applications of psychodramatic methods* (2nd ed.). New York: Springer.

Conyne, R. K. (1989). *How personal growth and task groups work.* Newbury Park, CA: Sage.

Corey, M. S., & Corey, G. (1997). *Groups: Process and practice* (5th ed.). Pacific Grove, CA: Brooks/Cole.

Donigian, J., & Malnati, R. (1997). *Systemic group therapy: A triadic model.* Pacific Grove, CA: Brooks/Cole.

Freire, P. (1970). *Pedagogy of the oppressed.* New York: Seabury.

hooks, b. (1994). *Teaching to transgress.* New York: Routledge.

Jacobs, E. E., Masson, R. L., & Harvill, R. L. (1998). *Group counseling: Strategies and skills* (3rd ed.). Pacific Grove, CA: Brooks/Cole.

Kees, N. L., & Jacobs, E. (1990). Conducting more effective groups. How to select and process group exercises. *Journal for Specialists in Group Work, 15,* 21–29.

Kraus, K., & Hulse-Killacky, D. (1996). Balancing process and content in groups: A metaphor. *Journal for Specialists in Group Work, 21,* 90–93.

Lappe, F. M. (1990). *Building citizen democracy: A discussion tool.* San Francisco: Institute for the Arts of Democracy.

Myers, I. B., & McCaulley, M. H. (1985). *Manual: A guide to the development and use of the Myers-Briggs Type Indicator.* Palo Alto, CA: Counseling Psychologists Press.

Napier, R. W., & Gerschenfeld, M. K. (1983). *Making groups work: A guide for group leaders.* Boston: Houghton Mifflin.

Palmer, P. (1987). Community, conflict and ways of knowing: Ways to deepen our educational agenda. *Change, 19,* 20–25.

Trotzer, J.P. (1989). *The counselor and the group.* Muncie, IN: Accelerated Development.

Tuckman, B., & Jensen, M. (1977). Stages of small group development revisited. *Group and Organizational Studies, 2,* 419–427.

Ward, D. (1993). An interview with Bob Conyne. *Journal for Specialists in Group Work, 18,* 99–108.

CHAPTER THREE

An Illustration of the Model for Task Groups in Action: The Action Phase

The action phase is represented in our model by two questions: "Who are we together?" and "What do we need to do to accomplish our goals?" The task of balancing process and content keeps the leader busy. This phase is a demanding one because it has characteristics of both the storming stage and the working stage of group work (Donigian & Malnati, 1997; Trotzer, 1989). It is a time when conflicting needs of members may emerge. Members want to appropriately differentiate themselves from others in the group yet remain connected to its larger goals and purposes. The predominant question is "Can I be myself and still be a member of this group?" The way in which this question is answered will influence each member's contributions and feelings about the group. It will also affect relationships between members and the leader and determine how cohesive the group becomes. The group can better accomplish its goals when members feel safe about expressing their personal views, while supporting others' needs for self-expression.

In Jane's professional organization meeting, acceptance of differing perspectives seems to be missing. Several questions come to mind regarding this scenario. Was the topic of difference put on the table? Were guidelines developed to help Jane and her members negotiate different views and work together collaboratively to resolve budget issues? From the little we know about Jane's group, we can see that something is missing. For example, did members have the opportunity to learn about each other's priorities and perspectives? Did members talk over each other in the meetings, or did they listen respectfully to differing viewpoints? It seems that the groundwork described in the warm-up phase was overlooked in this group, and explosions were one result.

The leader and member skills needed for the action phase of a task group include (1) using I-statements and speaking directly to others, (2) attending to the here-and-now, and (3) giving and receiving positive and corrective feedback. These skills were addressed in Chapter 1 and are especially crucial during the action phase, as closer examination will show.

We have already learned that it is important to model and encourage the use of I-statements during the warm-up phase. How we use language can shape dialogue and affect how people feel in relation to one other. Sklare, Keener, and Mas (1990) have some suggestions for leaders of task groups. When members talk clearly and directly to one another, communication is enhanced. For instance, it is important to remember that there are rarely any true questions; most questions are inverted declarative statements. Therefore, many questions are rife with hidden agendas that put receivers on the spot to defend themselves. Recall, for example, Jane's meeting, with its finger pointing and "why" questions. If the questioner asks himself, "Why am I asking this question?" and then answers, "Because. . . . ", he will reveal his hidden agenda or the true intention of the question. Thus, by changing questions into statements and reducing the use of "why" and "you," members may feel more receptive to the input of others, including the leader. In our task groups we often inform members that we will stop the conversation when they begin using "why" questions and words such as "we," "you," and "us." One of us used to ring a soft bell every time members lapsed into vague language. This response was helpful to members, although at times slightly frustrating and amusing, especially when the bell rang every few seconds. As members began to recognize the importance of clear language, however, their consciousness of this issue was heightened; and before long they were catching themselves or catching each other expressing ambiguous or harsh language. The leader was no longer the only person aware of the need for clear language and of its value to the work of the group.

The leader can also encourage members to pay close attention to how they speak to one another by referring to group guidelines and consensus statements developed by members. Consider this example:

◆

An instructor asked students to comment on how things were going in the class. One student jumped in with "Everything is fine; we are all having a good time." Immediately, two other students turned to the speaker and said, "No, we are not all having a good time. Since we agreed in our consensus statement to use clear language, please use I-statements when you speak about your own experience and express your views." These students offered the instructor feedback on changes they wanted in the class. Through a thoughtful discussion in which everyone then used clear language, all class members agreed to make some changes that included looking at each other more instead of the instructor and continuing their commitment to speak from their individual frames of reference.

In short, if leaders help members set guidelines early on for clear language, they will be able to monitor its use throughout the action phase.

Paying vigilant attention to the here-and-now and taking time to reflect on blocks that may be impeding the work of the task group are leader behaviors that can minimize withdrawing, attacking, and anger. One way to stay attuned to what is happening in the group is to engage process observers. Their role is to provide observations of content and process issues in a given task group meeting. It is not necessary that the leader and the members always agree with the process observations. Rather, they help the group pay attention to how things are happening and how the content is being addressed. Another example may provide clarity here:

In a previous session, a process observer had stated a view that several members disagreed with. During the next meeting these individuals looked at the process observer and proceeded to talk about him as if he were not present. The leader noticed this behavior and made a here-and-now group process observation: "There appears to be some strong reactions to what Bill stated in the last meeting. As we have noticed before, sometimes it takes a while for some of you to reflect on your reactions to what he states in his process observations. We agreed in our consensus statement to speak directly to one another and to make the effort to clear up unfinished business and address disagreements. I suggest we take a few minutes now to directly and clearly offer Bill feedback and reflection."

As the conversation continued, Bill was able to clarify his observations, while acknowledging that others might disagree with him. One of the members later commented that this incident taught her that people can disagree without being hurtful and disrespectful and can express disagreements and resolve misunderstandings within a climate of respect and caring.

In Jane's group, a process observer could have been a great resource for her and the group—a means for helping all of them understand what was occurring in the here-and-now and how to balance attention to both process and content.

The literature on counseling and psychotherapy groups underscores the value of feedback as a mechanism for helping people change and become aware of their impact on others (Yalom, 1995). While the purpose of task groups differs from that of therapeutic groups, members still must understand how they come across to others and how their behavior affects others because those interactions do have a bearing on group productivity (Campbell, 1996). In a task group the leader needs to pay close attention to the here-and-now to discover when behaviors, feelings, and attitudes get in the way of the group's progress. Then he can determine if or how these issues can be usefully addressed. If the leader takes time early in the life of the group to help members feel safe and comfortable about expressing different views and exchanging feedback, the group will reap great benefits in the action phase.

For example, recall the class situation in which members stated a view different from that of the member who said everything was fine. The ensuing exchange was successful in part because the class had spent time developing a consensus statement that supported open, direct communication. The class had also participated in a number of activities designed to identify ways in which members' preferences and styles differed. Finally, this exchange was successful because the leader was willing to convey an openness to feedback. When she asked, "Does anyone have any concerns about how I am running this class?" she communicated her genuine receptiveness to what members had to say.

Richard and Reverend Ellison have situations that will benefit from feedback. Richard can use feedback to bring attention to the interactions he observes in his faculty meeting. He might say:

I notice that there are two sets of viewpoints being expressed here, and I sense that it is hard for some of you to hear ideas that don't fit with yours. Let's stop and spend a few minutes finding out more about each other's current feelings and perspectives about English education. Such learning may help us continue our conversation more productively.

Through this intervention Richard acknowledges the unspoken differences and helps members slow down and reduce their dismissive reactions and rebuttals.

Reverend Ellison, as we noted in a previous chapter, sits through many interactions that are not related to the evening's task. As feedback, he might say:

◆

I notice lots of conversation, and I'm pleased that you have so much to share with one another. But I'm aware that time is moving along and we agreed to meet until 8:30 this evening. It is already 7:35, and we have yet to start on some important business items. As the leader of this meeting, I am feeling a bit anxious that we will not get our work done before many of you have to leave for other obligations. When we begin our reports, I am going to keep an eye on time; so please take only five minutes for your particular committee. I would appreciate it if you would let me know if we are not doing what we need to be doing in this meeting to make the evening productive and satisfying for everyone present.

If leaders model how to give and receive feedback, especially corrective feedback, they may enhance the likelihood that members will offer each other appropriate feedback (Hulse-Killacky & Page, 1994). Member-to-member feedback has been demonstrated to be most effective since members receive it more readily and with more influence from their peers rather than the leader (Yalom, 1995).

Balancing Content and Process

By shifting to the content arena, which must constantly be monitored in task groups, the leader helps the group brainstorm, consider options, put ideas into action, and achieve the goals for which the group was formed. Skills of cutting off, drawing out, holding the focus, shifting the focus, pacing and sequencing activities, clarifying, and summarizing all contribute to making this phase successful and productive. Recall Reverend Ellison's situation. He needs to help his members return to the reason for their meeting and make sure that all issues related to content are being represented. All the content issues present in the action phase are inextricably linked to a variety of interactions: leader with members, members with each other, and members with the group as a whole. Leaders may find certain skills and strategies helpful to their work at this phase; however, the biggest strength a leader can bring is an appreciation of the process and the knowledge that attending to "what is happening now" can provide clues and direction for effective task meetings (Heider, 1997, p. 27).

Consider Figure 3.1 as an example of a visual distortion in the action phase. See how the content line looms and the process line bobs up and down as if to say, "Notice me." Any number of things could be happening here. For example, people may feel disconnected from others or angry about something. They may be sighing, rolling their eyes, and giving various indications that the proverbial elephant is in the room but that no one is calling it by name. Often leaders in this situation are either unaware of or unwilling to address what is happening. Why? One explanation is related to the view that task groups are content-driven and participants often see no need to focus on process issues. In addition, task group leaders may not feel comfortable about addressing process issues because they do not have the skills to do so. As we noted in Chapter 1, leading any type of group involves using a range of skills to respond to complex situations. These skills can be learned, and with practice leaders can demonstrate competence and confidence. A leader's lack of attention to the here-and-now will likely result in a group that plows through content with no recognition of how process plays a role in the group endeavor. A common leader response to the situation illustrated in Figure 3.1 is "Come on, folks. Can we focus and get back to item 5 on the agenda? We only have 30 minutes left in this meeting." The leader may sense that something is awry, but his solution is to move further into the task, thereby ignoring or overlooking the process issue.

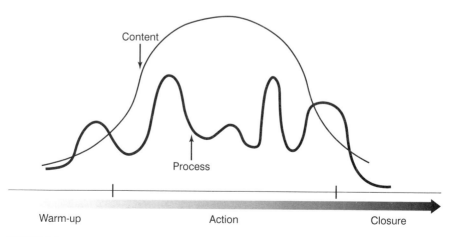

FIGURE 3.1
Reverend Ellison's situation: The leader's lack of attention to the here-and-now.

Reverend Ellison's church group meeting comes to mind as an illustration of the situation in Figure 3.1. He is committed to completing the agenda for the evening meeting yet seems oblivious to the many voices in the room. He chugs along without stopping to address what is going on around him. Note that the process line lingers after the content line has ceased; process insists on being recognized, identified, and addressed.

Like Reverend Ellison, Jane and Richard are in situations in which much is going on, both verbally and nonverbally, that indicates their need to stop and observe what is happening in the group. As Conyne (1989) notes, such blocks will eventually impede any substantive progress the group might make in achieving its purposes and goals. Reverend Ellison, Jane, and Richard all need to stop the action and observe that something is in the way. The group will benefit in the long run from the leader's patience in addressing these blocks. Often after the air has been cleared, task groups can move ahead with renewed vitality and commitment.

Figure 3.2 illustrates the struggle in Jane's group. Here the process line ceases in mid-action as the content continues like a slow bleed. The word *chaos* captures the battle lines drawn over budget decisions and the noise resulting from profound differences in perspectives, attitudes, and world views, and gives us a glimpse into Jane's internal struggle. She is unable to separate the *how* from the *what* in her meeting group. Unaware that she needs to untangle the process and content issues, she simply says (in effect), "I quit!" We can imagine her driving home wondering what she did wrong and why these members messed up her meeting.

There are two important points for leaders to recognize. First, if leaders believe that how things happen is as important as what happens in

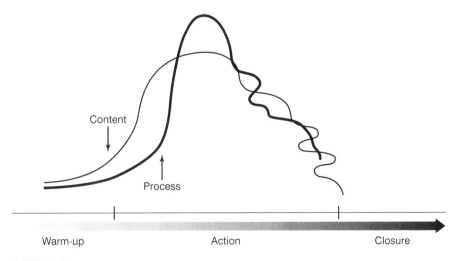

FIGURE 3.2
Jane's struggle: Disagreement to chaos: "I can't do this."

task groups, then they know blocks are an expected and normal part of a group's life. This recognition may help leaders focus on the here-and-now, an excellent tool to use when blocks occur. Second, task group leaders must understand that simply becoming aware of the here-and-now is not sufficient; the leader needs to act on that recognition. Figures 3.1 and 3.2 emphasize that leaders cannot take people into places where they will not tread themselves. If leaders are uncomfortable with conflict, are anxious when everyone does not agree, have concerns about being seen as attractive and competent, or are generally frightened about what might happen if people express their feelings directly, they must address those issues forcefully and soon. By examining their own feelings about conflict and feedback, leaders will increase their effectiveness and confidence in managing conflict and facilitating the exchange of feedback and differing views. While leaders can learn strategies and tips to guide their behavior, they cannot expect these tools to substitute for their own journey into understanding what is frightening about being in uncomfortable situations where people express anger and other difficult emotions. Donigian and Malnati (1997) make some points about confrontation that are readily transferable to task groups:

> As leaders, we need to be consciously aware that leader-to-member, leader-to-group, member-to-member, member-to-group, group-to-member confrontations will occur, sooner or later, as a natural part of the group's development. When people hear the word, confrontation, they usually envision individuals firing away at each other in a destructive, non-caring way. This should not be the practice of a group. Leaders have the responsibility to demonstrate the art and skill of confrontation and to reframe it as an act of grace and caring, so that members will see this intervention as a means for achieving greater intimacy. (p. 99)

In addition to intimacy, another important outcome in task groups is an enhanced level of goal accomplishment and more productivity. Consider again Jane's scenario. With some attention to differences, feedback, and a climate conducive for discussing competing viewpoints, Jane could help her group move beyond destructive communication to communication characterized by "grace and caring."

Action Themes

Several themes have emerged from our discussion of the action phase:

1. Attending to content

2. Recognizing conflict and exchanging feedback

3. Paying attention to the here-and-now and speaking in clear language

Once again we turn our attention to how our contributors reflect upon these themes.

Attending to Content

Mary Cathcart observes:

> The work of the labor committee (and all others too) is to hold a hearing in which the public can testify about proposed legislation. The committee has hearings one or two days per week, usually from 1:00 to 5:00 P.M., depending on the number of people wishing to testify. Six to eight bills may be considered per day. It is the responsibility of the chairs and the analyst to look at the bills, sort them by group or category, and then schedule groupings or categories on the same day so members of the public can testify on one day instead of having to come on several different occasions. This is fairly routine for all committees and results in a more efficient process.

> There are strict rules for conducting public hearings. We hear (1) testimony in favor of a bill, (2) testimony against a bill, and (3) testimony that is neither in favor nor against a bill. Individuals appearing before the committee are required to sign in; provide their names, addresses, and phone numbers; and identify if they are in favor or against and if they are speaking for themselves, a group, or an organization. During a large hearing, testimony is scheduled in time blocks with an hour for, an hour against, and an hour neutral. The senate chair presides, although most committees share the chairing assignment because members need to be at other commitments.

> Keeping up with the volume of commitments is a challenge. I have a great deal of conversation with the analyst and the house chair. There is simply not enough time for every work expectation because of multiple committee work. A hearing there involves lots of coming and going among committee members. Some may get bored or may not be interested in the topic, so they go do constituent work or something else. This can be very distracting for the public. It is difficult, but it is part of what happens.

The legislature is still a lay citizen body. A session is spread over
two years. The first year we meet for six months; the second we
meet for three. The salary is $18,000 for the session. Expenses in
the session are allowed up to $70 per day for food, mileage, and
lodging. Local work at home is not paid for. Other monies authorized, out of session, are for authorized committee meetings at
$55 per day, plus travel and lunch. There is also a constituent
allowance of $1,000 per year to cover postage, supplies, and
other expenses.

Don Reichard reflects on the action phase of the community college
coalition:

The group reviewed, revised, and adopted guiding principles:

Duplin County Leadership Center Guiding Principles
1. Principles of democracy, consensus, diversity, ethics, and
   accountability will be our operational norms.
2. The integration of new and existing leaders will be a central
   feature of our work.
3. Self-esteem, group development, and community change will
   guide the development and delivery of our leadership training.
4. Our training will include the development of our physical,
   mental, and intellectual abilities.
5. Our programs will be designed to respond to participants'
   needs and will enhance their leadership and decision-making
   skills.
6. Our programs will place a special emphasis on community
   application of skills learned.
7. Our programs will be nonpartisan.
8. Our programs will be inspired by global vision and the recognition that we are members of a worldwide community.
9. Our programs will be open to all members of our service area.
10. The center will work diligently to foster and practice commu-
    nication, cooperation, and collaboration with and among orga-
    nizations and groups in our service area.

These principles nicely capture the questions that appear in our model for
this phase: "Who are we together?" and "What do we need to do to accomplish our goals?"

Courtland Lee focuses on both process and content:

**Getting beyond "talking the talk" to "walking the walk":
Developing collaborative action plans to achieve strategic
outcomes**

To maximize effort, summit participants were divided into four
small working subgroups to begin brainstorming ideas for the
development of the multicultural agenda. These subgroups were
charged with continuing to assess the association's progress in
advancing multiculturalism and diversity and charting a course
for further action. Specifically, they were asked to consider ways
to operationalize goal C of the 1997–2000 ACA strategic plan:
"Diversity throughout the Association." They were encouraged to
think strategically and consider the long-term consequences of
their work. I told them that among the Iroquois, whenever a decision had to be made, the tribal elders would gather together and
first ask, "How will this decision affect our children 10 generations from now?" A facilitator/recorder was designated for each
group. The groups were given markers and newsprint and sent off
to work independently for most of the rest of the day.

Continuing small group work

During the morning and most of the afternoon, the participants
continued their work in the subgroups. In the early afternoon,
group 1 combined with group 2 and group 3 combined with group
4 to begin narrowing the scope of ideas being generated. The combined groups were asked to focus on common threads in their
ideas.

Large group processing

To further narrow the scope of ideas, near the end of day 2 the
participants reconvened as a large group to review the work of
the combined subgroups. By this time, each working group had
developed a draft of a multicultural/diversity agenda that represented the best ideas of the original subgroups. Working from
newsprint taped to the wall, the participants then worked to find
common threads among these two drafts. These commonalities
contributed to the formation of a rough document that represented the best ideas from all the subgroups. In a session characterized by a high level of energy, members decided that this document would start with a set of core values concerning issues of
multiculturalism and diversity and then state some basic principles. They also agreed that a set of goals and strategies would be
included.

By the end of the second day a rough multicultural/diversity agenda had been hammered out with significant contributions from each of the four original subgroups. Several participants volunteered to continue "wordsmithing" this document with a laptop computer after the group adjourned for the day. They promised to make photocopies of the document and have them available for the participants' review the following morning.

Finalizing the ACA multicultural/diversity agenda

As promised, copies of the draft document were distributed to participants in a large group session. In another lively group interaction, participants did final content editing on the agenda. After this editing, the participants unanimously adopted the document as the first draft of the multicultural/diversity agenda of the American Counseling Association. It was agreed that the document would undergo only stylistic editing over the next two months.

Larry Stokes reflects on his small business groups:

Regarding content, the leader assists by directing the brainstorming needed to develop a strategy to solve problems and begin the action phase. How group members work together during the action phase is every bit as important as what happens. Of course, we as a small business need to learn to live together in the workaday world. We can't forget that, once the report is written and delivered and the customer satisfied, we have to continue to solve other problems and complete other tasks together. The relationships that sell services and make a successful company are just as important as the relationships between each of the group members.

Issy Cross and Mary Frenning comment on the Sophomore Awareness Program:

After the opening session, all small group discussions are scheduled to follow major thematic presentations. The themes chosen are usually value-laden, opinion-provoking, and emotionally charged. Small group time, therefore, becomes increasingly useful.

John Phillips recalls:

In this particular group, the structure of the meetings helped assure that a clear purpose existed and process and content were balanced. Staff distributed information (content) to all board members weeks before the meeting. The meeting was always in a "public meeting" format: applicants for the certificate of need made their individual presentations followed by questions from the board and a staff analysis and recommendation. Then there was an open discussion with the whole board. This format, coupled with a balanced approach to content dissemination and a strong, attentive leader, kept the meeting functioning. Otherwise, there was the constant danger that either process or content would dominate the scene.

To prevent either process or content from dominating, it was necessary to (1) keep the focus of the group on the three issues earlier identified that surrounded the surgical center's certificate of need and (2) be certain that deliberation on the issues occurred openly, dispassionately, and thoroughly based on evidence that was accurate, balanced, and comprehensive and (3) make recommendations that were realistic, intelligible, and promote defined health goals.

Learning Points.   We have gained the following insights on content:

1. It is important to have a structure in place to facilitate the work of the group.
2. Visual aids and small subgroups can help get the task done.
3. Task accomplishment is enhanced by attention to process.
4. Providing information ahead of time helps prepare members for the task.
5. Brainstorming and generating solutions are helped by attention to how group members relate to one another.

Recognizing Conflict and Exchanging Feedback

Alice Cryer-Sumler pays attention to this theme in her children's groups. Here's an example:

> After the warm-up activity with group members, I sometimes used pictures or videos to move them into the working phase of our discussion groups. After group members shared what they observed in the picture, I asked them to share what they felt as they looked at the picture. Students shared an array of feelings such as anger, happiness, and frustration, to name a few. After

each student had an opportunity to share, ask another group member for clarification, and provide feedback, I helped group members make connections about the emerging themes. Group members were encouraged to recognize that their reflections could be different from those of others in the group.

Issy Cross and Mary Frenning recognize that a variety of opinions and reactions can surface in the Sophomore Awareness Group:

> The small group facilitators must determine the best way to process the variety of thoughts, reactions, feelings, and opinions that may surface from the large group discussion.

> Respect for individual differences within each group is requisite. Recognition of individual expression is encouraged. Requests for clarification and amplification of any topic are regarded as a responsibility of the co-facilitators.

Don Reichard continues on this theme:

> The issues statement was revised to read: "Development of leadership training and participation opportunities will enhance social/economic growth and improve the quality of life in Duplin County."

> In reviewing the coalition's history members were given opportunities to express their feelings about what they had learned so far. Differences in perspective among members could arise here, and any conflicts needed to be confronted and resolved.

> One member was concerned about the lack of able political leadership. The session leader recognized his opinion and reassured him that this subissue would eventually be addressed. It appeared that all members were comfortable about moving on.

> Later members were asked to suggest names for the leadership center since the word *institute* sounded too academic. To our surprise, a very spirited discussion developed, but members continued to respect each other and remained willing to listen to others' views. The names suggested were Duplin Leadership Academy, Duplin County Academy for Leadership Education, Duplin Leadership Center, and Dallas Herring Center for Leadership Development.

> In the third meeting the name topic was revisited. Pros and cons of each suggested name were solicited from members. Time was taken to let members reflect on the discussion and prepare to vote.

All had agreed previously to abide by the majority vote. A motion was made and approved to name the organization the Duplin County Center for Leadership Development.

Courtland Lee notes a moment during the multicultural summit in which differences came to light:

Large group processing

The participants reconvened for a brief large group processing session to end the first day. This gave them an opportunity to reflect on the day's progress and events. There was consensus that day 1 had been extremely provocative, powerful, and productive. The session revealed that each group was in a different place and had taken on a distinct character.

John Phillips offers another glimpse into his health planning group:

Given that the health planning process is loaded with potential conflict (numerous stakeholders and many dollars involved), I must ensure that all issues are addressed thoroughly and that all conflicting views receive adequate attention. I am dedicated to keeping the process as open and fair as possible. Otherwise, this public process would lose its credibility, and decisions would be continuously challenged. Moreover, board members are required to identify conflicts of interest. In such cases they can continue to discuss the issue but cannot vote on it, thus diminishing the conflict level.

Al Alcazar focuses on corrective feedback in his Bridging the Gap group:

Another incident in the group points to the complex and sensitive task of giving corrective feedback. At this particular meeting, we discussed the power of words—not so much in the traditional linguistic sense of words representing reality but in the postmodern sense of words creating reality. bell hooks (1994) says: "An unbroken connection exists between the broken English of the displaced, enslaved African and the diverse black vernacular black folks use today. . . . The poser of this speech is not simply that it enables resistance to white supremacy, but that it also forges a space for alternative cultural production and alternative epistemologies" (p. 171). The problem at this particular meeting centered on these "alternative epistemologies": if the "n" word is so abhorrent, why do so many African Americans use it among themselves? Listen to this exchange.

BRENDA: *(60ish black Baptist minister, a new group member)* I use the "n" word sometimes in jest and at other times to express affection. It is my way of disarming a racist term. I don't have any problems with it. But there's a whole load of problems when whites use the term. I mean. . . .

SEAN: *(white college sophomore, a new group member)* I am aware of the world of difference between whites using the "n" word for blacks and blacks using it among themselves. But if words do have power to create, aren't you doing the very thing you don't want us [whites] to do?

BRENDA: *(upset)* Listen here, young fellow. You worry about what your ancestors did to mine, and we can discuss semantics later on. . . .

I had to interrupt the exchange at this point. I had noticed a pattern in Brenda's response to white givers of feedback. The resulting emotional outburst always seemed disproportionate to the issue at hand when the corrective feedback came from a white person. (Expressions of feelings are encouraged in the group as long as they are not used as ad hominem attacks.) I then turned to another member of the group, a younger African-American law student, to bring us back to the point of discussion. Here's how Ed responded:

ED: I agree with Brenda about our [blacks] use of the "n" word. It really is our way of taking the horrible sting out of this word. I used to use it a lot, but now that I have children I make extra efforts at avoiding its use. But here's where I agree with Sean. This word does create a reality I don't want for my children. Maybe, as we distance ourselves as a nation from the ugly historical referent of the "n" word, we can eliminate its use completely.

Ed's words were not only beautiful and timely but had such a diluting and calming effect on the emerging conflict between Sean and Brenda that they apologized to each other for their respective share in the negative direction of the conversation.

Learning how to give and receive corrective feedback is essential for successful participation in all sorts of group work. But the leader in an "undoing racism" group must be an expert in the use and detection of the six factors identified in the Corrective Feedback Instrument (Hulse-Killacky & Page, 1994) that are involved in exchanging corrective feedback. Brenda's reaction to Sean's feedback had to do with a somewhat modified childhood memories factor with a heavy dose of reaction to the openly racist culture of her youth. It was as if she were saying: "Because my childhood memories of corrective feedback are negative ones from mostly racist white teachers, I am very sensitive about receiving corrective feedback from most whites now." Ed essentially agreed with Sean but did not—could not—trigger the childhood memories factor in Brenda that Sean did because of differences in historical power locations. This, of course, does not mean that a white person cannot give a person of color any corrective feedback. It simply means that people belonging to the dominant race must clearly show themselves to be undertaking the long and difficult journey of undoing racism in the process and content of the group.

Learning Points.   Several important learning points emerge from this section on recognizing conflict and exchanging feedback:

1. When members are given the opportunity to express feelings about the content, negative reactions are diffused.
2. Taking time to hear viewpoints that are in favor, opposed, or neutral helps all members feel heard and respected for their views.
3. Taking time to reflect on the work of the group reveals the many avenues people use to come to their conclusions.
4. Providing an open and fair process facilitates task accomplishment.
5. Leaders play a pivotal role in addressing conflict and facilitating the exchange of difficult feedback.
6. Leaders activate their executive function skills when addressing conflict and promoting the exchange of feedback.

Paying Attention to the Here-and-Now and Speaking in Clear Language

Larry Stokes reflects on this theme by emphasizing the need to be aware of what is happening in the group while it focuses on its work:

> With deadlines and schedules comes stress. Sometimes the pace gets so frantic that during the action phase some members in the group are likely to get angry and react. One of the tasks of the

leader in the action phase is to make sure that the energies of all members are channeled toward the end result. The leader, in a sense, becomes a process observer, observing the processes and interactions of the group members.

Issy Cross and Mary Frenning also consider the idea of the leader as process observer as they reflect on the Sophomore Awareness Program. They support the notion that leaders pay close attention to what is happening in the moment:

Facilitators are given a repertoire of techniques designed to encourage a balance of process and content. Co-facilitators are reminded to become conscious of the dynamics of individual group roles because they may assist or impede the process of group discussion.

John Phillips continues:

With any group, particularly a very diverse one with many stakeholders, there is a tendency to follow a historical path (this is the way it has always been done) or a train of thought that leads away from the issue under consideration. The leader of the group needs to keep the focus on the here-and-now of the issue. Otherwise, the work will never get done in a timely manner, and members may lose interest or become frustrated about the lack of meaningful progress. There is no question in my mind that the leader's failure to keep the focus on the here-and-now is very destructive to the group's work.

Al Alcazar also recognizes the importance of the here-and-now:

All of us have prejudices; but not everybody can inject them into procedures, policies, institutions, or systems that affect people's lives. When the latter happens, prejudice becomes racism. This is a controversial definition of racism, for it implies that only members of the dominant race in a certain region or country (insofar as they control the power in a given situation or location) can be racists. For the most part, this concept is not too difficult to understand; however, when it is linked with the idea of privilege, of white privilege in this country, the difficulty increases exponentially. Here's part of a conversation in the Bridging the Gap group:

KEITH: *(white college senior and group student leader)* A brief and honest look at our history will easily tell us who controls the economic and political power in our land. We have arranged everything in our society for our benefit and relegated people of color to the status of second-class citizenship. All whites benefit from this scheme of things in the sense that we are born into these beneficial arrangements. These, in turn, create a consciousness which we take for granted that we are "the better race"; and whether we admit to it or not this attitude of superiority saturates our dealings with people of color. It is in this sense that I say all whites are racists, and the only way out for us is to own up to our racism and. . . .

KIM: *(body language clearly indicating her growing resentment; after Kevin says, "born into these beneficial arrangements," she stops listening and soon interrupts)* So this means I am a racist just because I'm white? My family and my friends are racists? This is just too much for me to handle. I'm not ready for this shit. *(She walks out of the room).*

This is one of those here-and-now situations that group leaders need to pay close attention to in the action phase. There were several points of concern here. (1) Essentially, what Keith said was right; but if the leader acknowledged that now, Kim would be left with no support. (2) Most of the people of color in the room and about half of the whites (who were group veterans) knew Keith was right; but to let them express their agreement would have further alienated Kim and the rest of the new white participants who felt like her. (3) Kim's anger came from the way she interpreted Keith's words, and the phrase that cued me to her position was "just because I am white." This third point was the crucial here-and-now issue.

I asked Kim to stay for a moment. I assured her that all I wanted to understand was the reason for her anger, that it would help us tremendously with our work if she could tell us why she was leaving. Afterward, she could still leave. She sat down. She felt understood when I acknowledged that Kevin's comment sounded like white bashing. I explained that racism is not inherent in white people. I told her that after World War II Filipinos treated the Japanese with disdain and that for a long time Philippine laws clearly discriminated against the Japanese. I also recalled that Idi Amin made it illegal for all Asians to live in Uganda and expelled all Asian-Ugandans from his country. Racism has to do with prejudice and the ability to put prejudice in structures of power.

Kim stayed and eventually became one of the leaders of the group. That particular incident led to several considerations. First, we realized that, while our analysis of racism was accurate, it did imply that racism was inherent in whites. Without changing the definition, we had to put more emphasis on a dominant society's access to power and its ability to embed structures of power with prejudices (racism). Second, we had to write into our rules the need to see conflict and differences as essential to our work, that it was okay for Kim to turn to Keith and say, "That makes me really angry because it sounds like white bashing." Third, in race relations work, leaders need to realize that there is not a single overarching solution for racism, that the wisdom of the group is needed for each local issue that confronts them. This does not mean that we must be blind to institutional racism. Rather, we must be aware of the complexity involved in undoing such manifestations of racism. Fourth, the highly charged and subtle point about white privilege, which is at the heart of the misunderstanding regarding Affirmative Action, could not be effectively dealt with (content) unless the group had enough bonding (process) to contain or withstand its breaking or ungluing effects. This is one of the few, if not the only, instances in which the process line in Figure P2.1 should be slightly over the content line.

Larry Stokes comments directly about the here-and-now:

In my small business, once the warm-up phase had begun, the groups quickly moved into the action phase. It's evident that the members of the groups described in my business are frequently called on for quick and demanding action. These members have worked together for some time, and have learned to work together cooperatively. Although at times the pace gets very hectic, we try to remember to speak from our individual frame of reference and not blame others for those times when things go awry.

Learning Points.   Several points stand out concerning the here-and-now and clear language:

1. Leaders can attend to the here-and-now by serving as process observers.

2. Task groups are more productive when historical perspectives are minimized that interfere with the current purpose of the group.

3. Paying attention to body language and other nonverbal cues helps the leader be aware of how the behaviors in the group are helping or hindering goal accomplishment.

4. It is important for all group participants to speak from their individual frames of reference.

5. Clarity in language reduces ambiguity and the risk of being misunderstood.

Summary of Themes and Contributors' Reflections

Our contributors emphasize the importance of having a clear structure for the group's work. In both Don Reichard's and Courtland Lee's groups, there are mechanisms in place to ensure that attention to the content is clear and focused and that all members have an opportunity to be active in the group's work. The use of subgroups combined with large group reporting maximizes the possibility of member involvement. In addition, through such structures members have the chance to fully express their feelings and reactions to the task at hand. Issy Cross and Mary Frenning believe that students' opportunity to shape their own agenda is a key point of the Sophomore Awareness Program, while Mary Cathcart shows that a legislative group requires a clear and formal structure for public hearings.

What is illuminated through the contributors' stories is their respect for the group process. Even Mary Cathcart comments on issues that she would like to see addressed in legislative groups, such encouraging members to stay for entire hearings. She makes good use of her relationships with other committee chairs and the analyst to strengthen her positive influence as a leader.

John Phillips, Courtland Lee, Larry Stokes, Al Alcazar, Don Reichard, Issy Cross, Mary Frenning, and Alice Cryer-Sumler make it explicit that they value the relationships in their groups. They employ a number of interventions and strategies to stay aware of nonverbal behaviors, to encourage clear and direct communication, and to foster the appropriate and sensitive expression of feedback and differing views. Issy and Mary show that attention to diversity is actively addressed, not only by the trained co-facilitators but also by student group members in the Sophomore Awareness Program. While they maintain a strong focus on "Who are we together?" they never lose sight of the group's mission. In short, all our contributors believe that a leader must understand what her group needs to do to accomplish its goals. They seem to agree with Conyne (1989), who asks leaders to recognize and help remove blocks impeding the accomplishment of goals in task groups. They demonstrate their belief in Heider's (1997) message: "pay attention to what is happening now" (p. 27).

Don Reichard recalls the action phase in his group:

From a process perspective, the checklist for leaders and the agenda setting tools were used very effectively. Since the leaders were already trained facilitators, their use of these tools occurred naturally. (Compare the seemingly effortless swing of a professional golfer to mine!)

Conflict resolution and, at times, the creation of conflict to get members to speak were well managed. For example, the hidden agenda of one member to attack the poor leadership, in his opinion, of the county commissioners was recognized and overcome immediately. The member was made to realize that the situation was a long-term problem. Possibly, through some leadership opportunities offered in our center, more citizens with excellent leadership skills would eventually run for local office.

The coalition meetings were planned to allow time for reflection. The recurring theme that emerged was a feeling of frustration that the creation of a leadership center could not occur overnight. The group reluctantly accepted the fact that limiting factors included the lack of fiscal resources and the lack of time college staff could devote to the creation of the center since they were busy wearing other hats. But the college president assured the group that, even though progress might be slow, the center's development would progress steadily—and it did.

Emotion was also used effectively during the action phase. Time was taken, for example, to let members make impassioned remarks about the name of the organization at the second and third meetings. Emotions ran high because the name was going to have a great deal of symbolic meaning. Once the name was decided on, an obvious group sigh occurred, followed by a period of silence, allowing group members to collect themselves and realize that everyone must come together in support of our new name.

From a content perspective, decisions about the use of small groups, brainstorming, nominal group techniques, and so on were preplanned. Again, this was not a difficult task because all the leaders had been trained previously. We moved from developing the broad areas of mission and principles to the more specific areas of a name and a plan of action. This progression took place because the potential products had been envisioned by the leaders and the steering committee before the coalition first met. However, we had not envisioned the content of the products, only their general structure. The leaders were also well prepared to pay close attention to both process and content during the work sessions.

Suggestions for Managing Complex Issues in the Action Phase

By addressing the following points, leaders can become clearer about where they stand on issues of conflict, difference, and feedback. Through this type of exploration they can learn their strengths and limitations with regard to these issues. Once they have identified these points, leaders can take steps to refine their strengths and take part in whatever activities are required to help them become more comfortable with these issues. As a result, they will be more competent and confident in developing creative ways to help their members address the issues. The following items could be very helpful to the fictional leaders in our six scenarios. They also converge with many of the assumptions outlined in Chapter 1.

Checklist for Leaders

◆ Know yourself. Be aware of your own history about issues such as rejection, abandonment, conflict, anger, and the need for approval.

◆ Use a variety of means to create an atmosphere of safety, trust, and openness by first considering what factors need to exist for you to feel safe, to develop trust, and to be open to other views.

◆ Introduce the concept of individual differences early in the life of the group and begin to integrate those differences with examples of similarities. Help members explore how their views are different and similar with regard to the task at hand.

◆ Encourage members to discuss how their background might influence their behavior, reactions, and perceptions in a group. How might their values and beliefs become visible as the task group continues over time?

◆ Encourage the discussion that difference does not mean better or worse; rather, difference can be viewed without a value referent.

◆ Encourage members to reflect on perceived differences with others and to focus attention on the sources of their own reactions to those differences.

◆ Provide an opportunity for group members to look at how their experiences and perceptions of difference change over time. Leaders can pay attention to how things happen in the task group and offer group process commentaries over time—for example, helping members recognize how their ability to listen to different views is changing.

Helping Members Learn to Give and Receive Feedback

As we have noted, the exchange of feedback is more than just knowing the steps; it is often perceived as a complex and emotional event. Corrective feedback is particularly challenging for many people because the feedback giver must (1) invite the receiver to thoughtfully examine a potentially problematic behavior or (2) request that the receiver change a behavior. The development of the Corrective Feedback Instrument (Hulse-Killacky & Page, 1994) was one response to the need to find ways to help people grapple with the topic of feedback. The instrument has six major factors with 55 items presented in a Likert format. Respondents circle the number that best represents their level of agreement or disagreement with each item. Response options include *strongly disagree, disagree, slightly disagree, slightly agree, agree, strongly agree.* Here are several samples from the instrument:

◆ *Leader factor:* refers to items that relate to leader behavior in the group that fosters member-to-member feedback.

"If I observed the leader reinforcing the giving of corrective feedback in the group, I would be willing to give corrective feedback more frequently" (p. 204).

◆ *Feelings factor:* refers to affective reactions that people have to giving and receiving corrective feedback.

"Giving corrective feedback to others makes me very uncomfortable" (p. 205).

◆ *Evaluative factor:* refers to an evaluative or critical tone that some people experience when giving and receiving corrective feedback.

"When I receive corrective feedback, I think I have failed in some way" (p. 205).

◆ *Group role factor:* refers to one's preference for giving and receiving feedback in a group or one on one.

"I prefer to receive corrective feedback in a group so I can check out the accuracy of the feedback with other group members" (p. 206).

◆ *Written feedback factor:* refers to one's preference for giving and receiving feedback in written or verbal form.

"When I need to give corrective feedback, I prefer to write it out" (p. 207).

◆ *Childhood memories factor:* refers to how one's memories of feedback as a child influence one's behavior in the present.

"Because my childhood memories of corrective feedback are negative ones, I am very sensitive about receiving corrective feedback now" (p. 207).

These and the remaining 49 items capture a broad range of issues that contribute to the complexity inherent in giving, receiving, and exchanging corrective feedback. Our six scenario leaders could use the Corrective Feedback Instrument to gain some baseline data regarding their members' views about feedback. They could learn when and where it is easier or harder for members to express feedback to others. Leaders could also discover under what conditions their members best receive corrective feedback. The key to success in using the instrument or other such tools is the time taken to discuss member responses to individual items and to reflect on what these responses may mean to their work in the particular task group. See Hulse-Killacky and Page (1994) for details regarding the development of the Corrective Feedback Instrument.

In addition, members can use items from a microlab developed by Hulse-Killacky (1996). The purpose is to provide a structure for members to examine their concerns and feelings with other members. Members are asked to respond to several questions and statements and to discuss their responses in pairs and small groups. Here are some sample items from the microlab on feedback:

1. When someone says to you, "I'd like to give you some feedback":

   What do you think?
   What do you feel?
   What do you do?
   What is your worst fear?

2. When you need to give someone corrective feedback,

   What do you think?
   What do you feel?
   What do you do?
   What is your worst fear?

3. Reflect for a moment on the following phrase and then complete this sentence: "Receiving feedback as a child meant for me . . . "

In our experience as leaders of task groups (including graduate classes, training sessions, and meetings), members tend to benefit from the chance to identify their own reactions and then to hear how others manage feelings and thoughts about giving and receiving feedback. Time is taken after each segment of the microlab to discuss similarities and differences in the larger group. The Corrective Feedback Instrument, the microlab, and, more recently, the Corrective Feedback Self-Efficacy Instrument (Page & Hulse-Killacky, 1999) offer task group leaders tools for putting the topic of feedback on the table in a way that helps the leader, the members, and the group as a whole operate more effectively in the action phase. While these feedback tools were designed for use with students in graduate-level counselor training groups, they have much greater scope for providing members and leaders in task groups with resources for exploring the complexity inherent in feedback delivery and receptiveness.

Here, we draw from the writings of Jon Frew (1986), who encourages leaders to move the group into the differentiation phase by inviting two sets of dialogue.

1. *Leader to members:* Go around the room and tell each member how you are different from them. (p. 97)

This statement could be slightly rephrased in Jane's monthly board meeting:

◆

We have had lots of conversation about funding needs for the agencies we represent. We are now ready to begin examining the reality of our budget situation. Before we do that, I want each of you to tell members how your views about funding needs are different from theirs.

Perhaps a thoughtful dialogue about what the differences are and where they are situated in each member's value system will help Jane facilitate the expression of differences in a way that reduces the likelihood of explosions.

2. *Leader to members:* Are there any questions or concerns about the way I am leading this group? (p. 97)

This is an excellent question for all our fictional leaders to ask. For example, Paul could use this question to help him assess whether he is on the right track with his ambivalent employees. In addition, for all task group leaders, this type of question shows that the leader is open to feedback and serves as a powerful tool for staying vigilant to the process and content balance in the group. We like both of these items because they invite an open and honest discussion of relevant issues. Their successful implementation depends in part on how effective the coalition-building effort was in the warm-up phase.

To close this section on feedback, we refer our readers to Day (1981) as another resource that leaders can use to provide attention to differences. Unlike the activities presented in the warm-up chapter for introducing differences, Day's activity requires a level of self-disclosure and risk taking that seems more appropriate for the action phase. The activity also addresses the question "Who are we together?"

Members are invited to disclose information about themselves that taps something welcoming that they bring to the group as well as something that could hinder the work of the group. Through discussion of these qualities or behaviors, the group as a whole develops a greater awareness of the resources, gifts, and limitations that each person brings to the task group initiative. Members can draw, write, or verbally express an example of something welcoming and something to beware of. Maria's recreation committee comes immediately to mind here because she anticipates many different degrees of verbal participation with a broad representation of community members. Through this activity she might help members discover behaviors that can enhance the group's charge and those that might limit the work of the group.

One of the authors of this book worked with a school board when a variation of the welcome/beware activity was used. Board members met at a member's cottage one sunny afternoon. They were asked to go outside the cottage and locate items that represented (1) a strength that the person brought to the school board effort and (2) a hindrance to the work of the board. When members reassembled, they were asked to show their items and to discuss what they represented. As each member talked, time was given for others to comment and react. In one case, one member responded to another, "Now I know why you hang on to an idea so strongly. You really don't like to let go of your position." This individual had used a rock as an item representing both a strength and a hindrance. He was "solid as a rock," which had two meanings. On the one hand, he could be counted on; he was a "solid" member. On the other hand, he had definite views and opinions about certain topics; and like a rock, he wasn't about to budge. This exercise, accompanied by thoughtful and appropriate discussion, provided another avenue for members to better understand each other's world views and perspectives. All felt more connected to other members and better able to demonstrate empathy for positions different from their own.

Agenda Setting

Agendas can be another tool for leaders in the action phase. As Yalom (1983) suggests, agendas can be helpful in formulating the focus for a particular group. His agenda format invites each member to respond to the following points, which can be adapted for use in a single task group meeting:

What I want to accomplish today

What I need to do to accomplish my goal

The resources in the group that can help me

How I will know if I accomplished my goal for today

Again, our six scenario leaders would find these statements useful in charting the direction for their respective groups. Gladding (1999) observes that group members can often recognize their accomplishments when they formulate their goals at the beginning of each group session.

For many organizations and groups, the agenda is a major means for communication about meetings and what participants can (and cannot) expect to occur. In less formal situations, the agenda may be created at the beginning of the meeting. More frequently, especially for formal meetings, an agenda is created before the meeting. For participants to believe they have a useful role to play in meetings, some important questions about the agenda need to be clearly answered:

1. Who actually creates the agenda?
2. How does a participant get an item on the agenda?
3. When, in advance of the meeting, do agenda items have to be submitted?
4. Is the agenda sent to participants in advance of the meeting?
5. Is there a procedure for adding items to the agenda after it has been prepared?

If the answers to these questions are known to all concerned, then there is significantly higher potential for successful meetings and participation in them. If participants are not made aware of these answers, then there is a likelihood of disinterest, apathy, lack of participation, and disenchantment.

As we have noted throughout this chapter, the action phase is concerned with both content and process. Leaders are challenged to attend to the complex issues surrounding conflict, the expression of differing views, and the giving and receiving of feedback. By being vigilant in their attention to these process issues, leaders will assist their members and the group as a whole to more effectively and efficiently address matters related to content.

Final Tips for Leaders During the Action Phase

1. Continue to help the group address issues of differences, conflict, and feedback so that conversation is relevant to the work of the group and meaningful to members.

2. Use activities and exercises that help members recognize, listen to, and appreciate differences.

3. Continue to encourage I-statements.

4. Pay attention to the here-and-now of member interactions.

5. Model the giving and receiving of positive and corrective feedback.

6. Use agendas and other such tools to keep group members focused on the group content.

7. Provide a variety of structures (for example, subgroups) to facilitate member interaction and involvement in task group activities.

◆ ◆ ◆

Points to Ponder

1. Conflict is inevitable in a task group. Explain how a leader can address conflict to remove barriers to meeting the group's purpose.

2. Keeping the group focused on the here-and-now serves an important function in task groups. Explain what this idea means to you when you lead a task group.

3. During the action phase of task groups, leaders are often vulnerable to pushing to achieve the goal without giving enough attention to process issues. Explain how this inattention to process can actually block goal achievement.

4. Leaders are expected to take a lower profile in the action phase of task groups as members assume a more active role. At the same time, leaders are expected to be more attentive to process and content issues. Explain how you might balance these two leader expectations in your task groups.

◆ ◆ ◆

References

Campbell, L. (1996). Samuel T. Gladding: A sense of self in the group. *Journal for Specialists in Group Work, 21,* 69–80.

Conyne, R. K. (1989). *How personal growth and task groups work.* Newbury Park, CA: Sage.

Day, R. W. (1981). WELCOME/BEWARE: A structured activity for use in the initial stages of counseling and therapy groups. *Journal for Specialists in Group Work, 15,* 30–36.

Donigian, J., & Malnati, R. (1997). *Systemic group therapy: A triadic model.* Pacific Grove, CA: Brooks/Cole.

Frew, J. E. (1986). Leadership approaches to achieve maximum therapeutic potential in mutual groups. *Journal for Specialists in Group Work, 11,* 93–99.

Gladding, S. (1999). *Group work: A counseling specialty* (3rd ed.). Upper Saddle River, NJ: Merrill/Prentice Hall.

Heider, J. (1997). *The tao of leadership.* Atlanta: Humanics New Age.

hooks, b. (1994). *Teaching to transgress.* New York: Routledge.

Hulse-Killacky, D. (1996). Microlab on feedback exchange (Unpublished document).

Hulse-Killacky, D., & Page, B. J. (1994). Development of the Corrective Feedback Instrument: A tool for use in counselor training groups. *Journal for Specialists in Group Work, 19,* 197–210.

Page, B. J., & Hulse-Killacky, D. (1999). Development and validation of the Corrective Feedback Self-Efficacy Instrument. *Journal for Specialists in Group Work, 24,* 37–54.

Sklare, G., Keener, R., & Mas, C. (1990). Preparing members for "here-and-now" group counseling. *Journal for Specialists in Group Work, 15,* 141–148.

Trotzer, J. P. (1989). *The counselor and the group.* Muncie, IN: Accelerated Development.

Yalom, I. D. (1983). *Inpatient group psychotherapy.* New York: Basic Books.

Yalom, I. D. (1995). *The theory and practice of group psychotherapy* (4th ed.). New York: Basic Books.

CHAPTER FOUR

An Illustration of the Model for Task Groups in Action: The Closure Phase

The closure phase is a critical time in the life of a task group. It is the time when members should pull together what they have learned so that their learning can be transferred beyond the group experience. Conyne cautions, however, that leaders and members can get so caught up in an experience that they see the group as the "end-all for the whole experience" (cited in Ward, 1993, p. 106). They fail to recognize that "group participation really is meant to be a time-limited experience to help people to get from here to there" (p. 106). In other words, task groups are organized around specific goals, and membership is required for the time it takes to complete them. Then the group ends. The challenge for task group leaders is to provide time for reflection about not only what has been accomplished but also how the goals have been addressed. In therapeutic groups, attention is commonly given to helping members reflect on what they have learned, how they have changed, and how the relationships in the group have contributed to the learning that has occurred (Corey & Corey, 1996; Donigian & Malnati, 1997; Gladding, 1999; Hulse-Killacky, Kraus, & Schumacher, 1999). Such reflection is useful for task groups as well.

Closure in task groups presents some notable challenges. For example, whether looking at a single group meeting or meetings over time, we find that the product or goal orientation in task groups makes it hard to recognize reflection time as a significant part of the group's purpose. However, without pausing and reflecting on both process and content, members cannot make important connections between their experiences in the group and life after the group. Task group participation gives individuals the opportunity to learn to cooperate and collaborate with each other and to enhance their ability to participate as effective citizens in other areas of life (Ettin, 1993). As Hulse-Killacky et al. (1999) note, "the task/work environment provides an opportunity to address the task while learning how to identify, understand, and develop empathy for differing worldviews, work styles and needs" (p. 122). Implicit is the need to provide time for members to focus on how their participation in the concluding task group may have an impact on their work in future task groups.

In addition, members frequently come and go in task groups. People arrive late and leave early, making it hard for leaders to help them reflect on the learning that has taken place for individuals, for members in relation to one another, and for the group as a whole (Donigian & Malnati, 1997). Consider Letitia's legislative education subcommittee meeting. She is concerned that members have not addressed the budget decisions, and her concerns are heightened by the abrupt departure of two members, who basically get up and leave. Letitia has no chance to learn about their reactions to the meeting and, equally important, what they plan to do to prepare for the next meeting. She is unable to address the question that captures both process and content in the closure phase: "What outcomes resulted from this task group experience?" Embedded in this question is attention to accomplishments and next steps as well as how the relationships in the group enhanced or hindered the task. Leaders of task groups need to understand that the closure phase is part of the group's work, not something to add or leave out depending on time. Figure 4.1 captures a moment similar to the one in Letitia's group. Looking at the figure, we can almost hear her lament, "Don't leave and do this to me!"

Notice how the balance between process and content is quickly disrupted and how both lines seem to fizzle out in midair. We can imagine the following conversation:

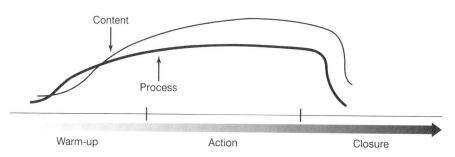

FIGURE 4.1
Letitia's lament: "No, please wait! We are not finished here yet."

MEMBER: I have to go now

LEADER: Oh, I didn't know you were leaving early. Well, okay, good-bye.

This dialogue illustrates a common scenario in task groups. The challenge is for leaders to see endings as central to a successful task experience. Without a clear sense of closure and time for reflection, group participants will leave without understanding what happened, how it happened, what worked, what did not work, and what next steps need to be considered related to the purpose of the task group. Although leaders cannot control late arrivals and early departures, they can design structures to maneuver through these disruptions. For example, Letitia could have stopped the action of the group and said:

> I am sorry you both have to leave. However, please stay for just a few minutes more so we can all get some sense of where we go from here. I really would like some quick feedback from you on two areas. First, as you can see, we still have these budget decisions to make. How shall we proceed? What can I count on having you do between now and our next meeting? Second, I would like to know how the meeting worked for you today. Is our structure helping you participate and helping us as a group meet our goals?

In this statement, Letitia is letting her group members know that she needs some type of closure from them—some feedback on the task and on how the group is going about its work. After the two members depart, she can continue to discuss these items with the remaining members so that everyone is clear about what will happen next.

Endings are also important because they give everyone a chance to finish the work and feel a sense of completion. However, we offer a word of caution. Often group members who have not contributed to the work of the group suddenly feel a need to bring up unfinished business or private agendas. At these moments leaders need to engage their executive function skills and nip such conversations in the bud. Otherwise, full closure will not occur.

Consider another example of poor closure. We have a colleague who attended a series of public school faculty meetings that ended for the year without any attention to closure. Thus, when teachers returned in the fall, the first meeting seemed like a vague extension of the meeting that concluded in the spring. Imagine the task and process confusion and ambiguity that must have evolved from this situation.

The reality for those of us who convene and facilitate task groups is that members are usually busy with complicated schedules. For example, members may have jobs and families, meaning that their presence in the group is affected by their multiple roles and responsibilities. It is impossible to expect all participants to be present at the same time. Thus, the goal of closure is not to create a perfect situation but to give the concept of closure the importance it deserves and to help participants feel a sense of completion. The topic of closure must be included in the warm-up phase discussions of group norms or guidelines. If closure is seen early on as part of the structure of the group rather than a separate activity or a luxury, then members will recognize its importance and be more open to engaging in activities that promote appropriate and meaningful closure. For example, Letitia could follow the guideline of providing some type of closure for each legislative meeting, regardless of whether or not members have to leave early. If members know from the beginning that "we will review both our goals and next steps as well as examine how the group participation is helping or hindering the work of the group," Letitia will surprise no one when she stops the action and reviews these points with members who have to leave early. Remaining members will have their chance to obtain closure at the regular time and will do so with some clear information about their colleagues' feedback and observations. Thus, ambiguity and disorder will be minimized.

Closure is directly related to accountability. When groups work well, leaders need to know how and why they work well so that certain strategies, models, and structures can be repeated in future groups. If groups do not work well, leaders can learn to design more effective task group meetings in the future. In her exploration with members Letitia may find that certain activities really seem to help the group meet its goals. She may also find that other members have noticed that the group sometimes gets off track and into other issues that are not germane to that particular meeting's goals. The fact that much conversation on nonbudget issues was occurring just before the two members got up to leave indicates that Letitia and her group need to pay more attention to priority items before they become distracted by other issues. Pausing and reflecting on both the process and content of the group meeting can be helpful tools for preventing wayward conversations.

Finally, attention to closure provides another benefit to the task group: applause. Group members who work hard together to successfully accomplish goals need time to applaud their individual and collective efforts. Robert Schumann, the great Romantic composer, once observed that "everyone needs applause." Sharing positive feedback and appreciation can buoy a group's spirits and remind members of Sam Gladding's words: "time after time I realized it was relationships between group members that either made or unmade the productivity in groups I led or in which I participated" (cited in Campbell, 1996, p. 74).

When the relationships contribute to the success of the task group, then time needs to be given to celebrate that type of experience. If leaders and members work together to create climates that foster and nurture communication, cooperation, and collaboration, then it is equally important to take time to reflect on the task group experience in terms of the group's strengths and shortcomings.

Al Alcazar writes:

> The public school system in New Orleans is a major source of anguish and frustration for many children and parents caught in and thrown into the system by forces (mostly economic) beyond their control. There are, of course, a few public schools that are exceptional. For several years now I have observed a diverse group of parents camping in line, sometimes for a week or two, rain or shine, so that their children can get into this excellent city elementary school. As a founding member of the Jeremiah group (we take our mission and vision from the words of Jeremiah, who said, "Seek the peace of the city, for in its welfare you will find your own"), I was excited about the possibility of doing something about the public school problem. I had heard so many people complain that I lost my tolerance for complainers. To every complainer, I would say: "If you're not doing anything about it, you're part of the problem." This was how the Jeremiah group was formed. The idea was really simple. If we can create a community willing to establish strong relationships to do grassroots democracy in the prophetic tradition of Jeremiah, we can create 10 excellent public schools, just like the one people line up for, every 10 years.
>
> Because of the emphasis on strong relationships in the Jeremiah group, we carefully attend to the warm-up and action phases. However, we also pay meticulous attention to closure. In our meetings there is an almost fanatical insistence on being on time: we start on time and end on time. This insistence has multiple benefits for the warm-up phase but more so for the closure phase. Closure is structured into every meeting. When the meeting looks as if it will go beyond the planned time, the leader interrupts the agenda and asks for everyone's approval for an extension.

Al's focus on time reminds us of Reverend Ellison's dilemma. Recall that his church group wandered through various topics; but just as the members were beginning to discuss agenda items, they began getting close to the ending time. People were shifting in their chairs, looking at the clock, and planning to depart. Reverend Ellison could benefit from the structure used in the Jeremiah group: setting a norm of starting on time and ending on time. Realizing that no meeting works perfectly, he could refer to that structure as the time approached 8:30 by asking everyone's approval for an extension. If some were willing to stay, those who had to leave could be asked to comment on what they were prepared to do to meet certain goals and to prepare for the next meeting.

Closure Themes

Four major themes have emerged from our preceding discussion on closure:

1. Reviewing goal accomplishment
2. Preparing for future activities
3. Reviewing the impact of group relationships on goal accomplishment
4. Expressing appreciation

Reviewing Goal Accomplishment

Mary Cathcart discusses the legislative hearings:

There is a work session for each piece of legislation:

◆ The analyst summarizes the bill and notes the pluses and minuses.

◆ The committee discusses.

◆ A question is asked: "Is more information needed?" Proponents and opponents may be present and can be called on at the discretion of members.

◆ A question is asked: "Should the motion (1) pass or (2) not pass?"

◆ Discussion occurs and then a vote resulting in (1) pass, (2) not pass, or (3) a divided bill.

◆ If the result is (1) pass or (3) a divided bill, the bill goes to the House or the Senate for consideration. The Senate chair leads the debate in the Senate; the House chair takes this role in the House.

Don Reichard reflects on several coalition meetings:

At the end of the first meeting, members indicated that there was a great need for a leadership institute in Duplin County. At the end of the third meeting, a leader covered major points with participants. He said a Duplin County Center for Leadership Development steering committee had been formed with members consisting of the committee chairs and co-chairs, himself, and the college president. He asked if others wanted to serve, and some did. He explained that the steering committee would work over the next year to implement the plan of action. At an appropriate point, the coalition would be brought back together for a progress report and additional input.

Courtland Lee reports:

The summit ended with the participants first formulating a dissemination plan for the agenda both within and outside of the association.

Larry Stokes offers this observation:

In the small business setting, the closure phase is probably the element of the group model that gets the least amount of attention, perhaps because there is too much to do and too little time in which to do it. Closure is not given enough attention because of the need to go on to the next task. However, a group without closure is like a circle of people who watch a ball get thrown into the air that never comes down. People stand there looking up, holding out their hands, wondering what in the world happened? Why didn't the ball come down? The closure phase allows for a sense of completion—a review of what was accomplished so that this learning can be used in the future.

Concerning the Sophomore Awareness Program, Issy Cross and Mary Frenning observe:

Because the three-day awareness program is fast-paced and filled with many provocative topics, closure is imperative. It is useful at the end of each small group session and is especially helpful at the end of the full three-day program.

For students, the closure technique helps them review and reinforce the discussions that have occurred in the small groups and at the end of each session.

Alice Cryer-Sumler recalls the closure phase in one of her children's groups:

Students were invited to reflect on what they had learned or how they planned to use the experience and information from the session. Often I would present a sentence starter and ask the group members to complete the sentence. For example, I would say, "Please complete this sentence: 'Today I realized that. . . . '" By completing this incomplete statement, group members continued to process their learning.

Learning Points.   From our contributors we have learned the following:

1. Closure is important in task groups and hard to emphasize because of the heavy focus on content.
2. Without closure members may feel unsettled, unsure of what happened and why.
3. Reviewing what was accomplished helps members end their work in the group.

Preparing for Future Activities

Several of our contributors see a relationship between attention to closure and what happens in future groups. Larry Stokes reminds us that without closure there is no resolution to what happened in the group or clues about what to expect in the future:

> The closure phase is a time when members can pull together to review what worked and what did not work. What needs to be done to make a similar group work in the future?

Don Reichard offers another example of preparing for the future:

> In the first two sessions the leaders expressed how impressed they were with the plans that were shaping up for the institute's structure. They then outlined the plans for the third session and bid all of us good-bye.

Al Alcazar discusses part of the closure phase for the Jeremiah group:

> The first part of closure is a review of what participants need to do "out there" as a result of the commitment made "in here" at this particular meeting. One of the tasks, for instance, could be to contact a member of the school board who represents the school we would be working with and to schedule a meeting with that

person. The names of the group members who would attend and the agenda of the meeting would be quickly reviewed. Another person would record the discussion in the meeting with the school board member and would read the minutes at the next Jeremiah group meeting. Everyone would be clear on the commitments made to mark the end of the meeting.

Issy Cross and Mary Frenning demonstrate how their closure activities have an impact on future program design:

The finale of the three-day program is the presentation of student-designed skits. Each small group is asked to work on developing a vignette during specified times throughout the three days based on what they have learned. Students are also asked to provide their reactions to and reflections on the three-day experience. Students participating in the skits are asked at the end of their performances to give brief personal feedback comments about the Sophomore Awareness Program to the entire audience.

Students are also asked to fill out a formal evaluation instrument to provide feedback on the quality and effectiveness of the presentations, the impact of the small group discussion experience, and any other comments about the total program they may wish to make.

The finale for the co-facilitators is a "feet up" and "hair down" group process meeting. This time allows for individual and group closure on the intense work of the past three days. Program goals can be reexamined to determine the degree to which the originally proposed outcomes were realized. Often testimonials are given, recommendations for program improvement are offered, and commitment for future service to the program is volunteered. Co-facilitators are also requested to complete a formal evaluation instrument. The planning committee is asked to write a final summary report on the effectiveness and usefulness of the program for inclusion in the last high school newsletter of the year as well as in the district's year-end report to the community.

Learning Points.   A few observations are helpful to consider in the closure phase:

1. Taking time to close helps members anticipate future task group participation.
2. Providing reflection time gives members a clear plan for the next meeting.

Reviewing the Impact of Group Relationships on Goal Accomplishment

This point is often overlooked in task groups because of the frenetic focus on content and product. Our contributors offer some illustrations about how reflecting on the relationships in the task group during the closure phase can yield important information for group leaders to consider. Larry Stokes starts us off:

> I'm reminded of an example of a lack of closure through music. Music is a series of tension and releases. What would happen if tension was all there was and nothing was released to close out the song? Somehow I don't think that music would be so pleasant if it was all tension. The same goes for groups and teams. The closure phase is a time when members can pull together to review what worked and what did not work. What needs to be done to make it work in the future? What did each member do well so that the team was able to accomplish its goal and move on to the next?
>
> This description of closure indicates that groups end. In my business many groups begin and end during a workday. The closure phase allows for a sense of completion. It also allows for a review of what was accomplished so that this learning can be used in the future. The chance will arise again for groups in my setting to convene to solve other problems and accomplish other tasks. What has been learned before can be used again so that the group can be even more effective and successful.

In reviewing his group closure phase, "Deconstructing the Space," Courtland Lee provides more insight into the link between relationships in the group and goal accomplishment:

> The participants brought closure to the entire experience by sharing their feelings about the summit. Again, there was consensus that the summit had been an extremely provocative, powerful, and productive experience, both personally and professionally. What impressed many of those who attended was that the leaders who bonded together to develop the agenda demonstrated how they could come together, despite their different philosophies and work settings, to advance the profession of counseling. It was the hope of those who participated in the summit that the multicultural/diversity agenda would become an important strategic planning and policymaking document for ACA.

Don Reichard reflects on the first and second meetings of his coalition group:

The leaders, using the rounds closure technique, asked members to express their feelings on whether they had wasted their time, were glad they came, and would return to the next meeting. The answers were no, yes, yes! It was decided that there is a great need for a leadership institute in Duplin County. Members felt the session had been very successful but tiring. They said they were looking forward to the final one.

Al Alcazar notes a closing activity for the Jeremiah group:

In the first round, each participant indicated what aspect of the meeting made him or her uncomfortable and how that particular incident could have been handled better.

John Phillips considers how members pulled together what they had learned:

My first reaction to this focus was that it did not apply to my health care group since the final product of the process was a decision made. That was it! Yet it is clear that board members, all of whom are community and professional leaders, learned a great deal about the health care needs of the community and a complex process that has future ramifications for all health care facilities in the region. This knowledge now has intrinsic value in their own personal and professional lives, just as it has had an impact on my own thinking.

Issy Cross and Mary Frenning reflect:

Closure activities can help to summarize discussion content, acknowledge contributions of individual group members, recognize the respect given to differing opinions, and lead to group cohesiveness and positive interaction. However, facilitators should never feel so complacent that they fail to be alert to needs within the group that may still require attention. Although group process may have good closure, some students may require more discussion time on a particular topic and may want much later on in the program to revisit an issue or a topic already passed.

Learning Points.   Our contributors make several points about the impact of process on outcome:

1. Reflecting on what worked and did not work in the group provides direction for future task groups.

2. Reflecting on members' feelings about the group can help members discover how they accomplished a difficult task while acknowledging and working through individual differences.

3. Hearing members' feelings and reactions honors the work of the task group and helps provide a sense of completion.

Expressing Appreciation

Al Alcazar speaks for many of our contributors when he notes:

> The second closure round provides an opportunity for members to express support and delight over parts of the meeting that have gone well. The third part is a prayer of gratitude to the God we address in different names whose providence and care keep our organization working together on the difficult and complex task of seeking "the welfare of the city."

"Spirit" and "delight" capture the sense of applause that helps task members leave the group feeling that their presence made a difference. And the prayer of gratitude that Al describes shows that a group can have a sense of spirit that is indeed greater than the sum of its parts.

Learning Points

1. Taking time to express appreciation can raise the self-esteem of members in a task group.

2. The focus on applause taps into the spirit and magic of task groups that work well.

Summary of Themes and Contributors' Reflections

The rich illustrations from our contributors' stories accentuate the need for closure in task groups. Without closure leaders and members alike will not know how to proceed in the future. Taking time to review goal accomplishment also stands out in the stories. Reviewing tangible accomplishments gives closure to everyone and suggests ideas for use in future groups, as Mary Frenning and Issy Cross make clear. Applause can be given for a job well done. Equally compelling is the awareness that members are great resources for helping leaders understand what worked and what did not work. Our contributors provided members with the necessary structure and time to reflect on their participation in the group so that appreciation could be expressed as members concluded their work.

Alice Cryer-Sumler holds fast to her belief that however short a group experience might be in the school setting, time must be allocated so that group members can reflect on what has occurred and what they can usefully take away to their life outside the group. Her structured closure in a 45-minute children's group affirms the view that closure is a necessary part of the total group experience.

It is important to emphasize that closure in task groups is often hard to accomplish. The focus on content and goals is one reason as is a general sense that task groups are formed for work, not for attention to relationships and process. Clearly our contributors offer another perspective. For them, closure can be perceived by leaders and presented to members as a significant and vital component of the task group endeavor. The challenge is to find ways to introduce closure as a major part of task groups and to enhance its presence throughout the life of the group.

Alice Cryer-Sumler reflects on the closure phase with middle school children's groups:

> Some students found this phase of the group somewhat challenging because I asked them to respond to this question: "How are you going to use what you learned in this group today?" The question provided a framework for students to again be reflective. Reflections can be soothing because the mind has a focus and slows down a notch or two. In addition, closure allowed the students an opportunity to personalize the experience. The group only had 45 minutes to meet, with only 10 minutes given to the closure phase. Although I wished we had more time, in a school setting everything has a time limit. Even though the time during this phase was limited, the students did leave with a sense of closure to each group session.

Suggestions for Ending Task Groups

Rounds

We have several suggestions for rounds:

- Members can be asked to describe how they felt surprised by, delighted with, displeased by, or confused by today's meeting or the task group meetings over time.

- Members can be asked to name one thing they will take with them to use in their everyday life.
- Members can be asked to describe what they need to do to prepare for the next session or for future groups.
- Members can be asked to describe what worked for them and what did not work for them in the task group meeting.
- Members can be asked to talk about any appreciation or regret they feel now that the task group's work is ending.

All of these steps could be helpful to our six fictional group leaders. Paul, for example, wants some feedback on how his first session was received by his employees. Did he achieve his goals? He may hope that his workers will be delighted when they discover that what they most dreaded—touchy-feely time—did not happen. Rather, the time together was useful for helping everyone get on track for supporting the goals of the landscaping business. Similarly, Maria may discover that her recreation committee members were engaged in the task and enjoyed getting acquainted with other members of their community. If Maria did create a climate of equality and was able to hear from all group members, she could express her appreciation to everyone for attending and participating in a task that will benefit children in the community.

Letters to Members

This activity might be especially helpful to a task group that is taking a break from its regular meetings. Recall the school group that disbanded when the school year was over without any attention to closure. When the group reconvened the next fall, everyone felt confused because no real closure had occurred in the spring. The leader of that group could have provided some closure by asking members at their final spring meeting to write themselves a letter describing something they would be willing to (1) challenge themselves to do over the summer break, (2) think more about, or (3) try differently as a result of their role in the school. The letter activity conveys the point that life does continue beyond the group and that the learning members experience can be directly applied to their lives elsewhere. In this activity, members address an envelope to themselves and place their letter inside. The leader mails the letters five or six weeks after the task group ends. In the opening fall meeting, the leader could ask members to revisit their letters and reflections to make the transition into the new school year.

Richard might try this activity at the end of the school year as well. The letters may help his faculty members reflect on their membership in the group so that they come prepared in the fall to begin anew. Perhaps they will challenge themselves to pay attention to and appreciate the diversity that is represented on the English staff.

Transfer of Interpersonal Learning

We share Ettin's (1993) belief that as people work effectively in small groups they can garner skills for being more effective and influential in other groups. These groups can take place in local, state, national, and global settings. If the process truly works in task groups, then members will have some self-awareness and interpersonal skills to help them function more successfully as citizens.

For this activity, leaders can simply encourage a dialogue about the transfer of learning. For example, members can wonder if and how the relationship and connections in the task group have helped them achieve the goals for which the group was formed. Al Alcazar's reflection on "learning among strangers" versus "learning among neighbors" comes to mind. If the various process and content issues have been addressed throughout the warm-up and action phases of the task group, members can explore how interpersonal learning in the task group figures into other types of group experiences and how members can take what they have learned in their ending group to other places where people meet to solve problems and accomplish tasks.

As with feedback and conflict, leaders are encouraged to become aware of their own feelings about endings and closure and how they may directly (or indirectly) avoid attention to closure. Leaders may feel, for example, that the task goals dominate and that closure is not important. On the other hand, they may be reflecting their own discomfort about hearing people express feelings of loss and sadness when a task group ends. Some of our most powerful endings occur in classrooms where students have gathered over the course of a semester and have developed strong interpersonal bonds. In those cases there is always a mix of sadness about the ending and joy about what was accomplished and what new opportunities lie ahead. When group members take part in a task group in which they can accomplish goals, feel connected to others, and discuss issues that matter to them, they enjoy the chance to express what they have learned and appreciated. The role and power of interpersonal learning is an important concept for leaders and members to include as they prepare to end a task group.

Final Tips for Leaders during the Closure Phase

1. Help members review and assess their work in the task group so that they have a plan about how to prepare for future meetings and other task groups.

2. Help members consolidate their interpersonal learning in the group. How did the work get done? How did the relationships in the group help or hinder the goal accomplishment?

3. Help members understand how interpersonal learning in the task group can transfer to action beyond the group—to their local and extended communities.

4. Help members see the task group for what it was and to gain closure with the current experience.

5. Help members express their appreciations and regrets and say good-bye.

◆ ◆ ◆
Points to Ponder

1. Explain what makes closure an important phase in a task group.

2. Explain why leaders of task groups need to have a clear concept of how they want their task groups to end.

3. Explain the effect that late arrivals and early departures can have on (a) the task group process during the closure phase of an individual task group meeting and (b) the end of the entire task group experience.

4. Explain how closure is related to accountability in a task group and what gives closure value.

5. Explain how closure and applause are related in task groups.

◆ ◆ ◆

References

Campbell, L. (1996). Samuel T. Gladding: A sense of self in the group. *Journal for Specialists in Group Work, 21,* 69–80.

Corey, M. S., & Corey, G. (1997). *Groups: Process and practice* (5th ed.). Pacific Grove, CA: Brooks/Cole.

Donigian, J., & Malnati, R. (1997). *Systemic group therapy: A triadic model.* Pacific Grove, CA: Brooks/Cole.

Ettin, M. F. (1993). Links between group process and social, political, and cultural issues. In H. I. Kaplan & B. J. Sadock (Eds.), *Comprehensive group psychotherapy* (3rd ed., pp. 699–716). Baltimore: Williams & Wilkins.

Gladding, S. T. (1999). *Group work: A counseling specialty* (3rd ed.). Upper Saddle River, NJ: Merrill/Prentice Hall.

Hulse-Killacky, D., Kraus, K. L., & Schumacher, R. A. (1999). Visual conceptualizations of meetings: A group work design. *Journal for Specialists in Group Work, 24,* 113–124.

Ward, D. (1993). An interview with Bob Conyne. *Journal for Specialists in Group Work, 18,* 99–108.

◆

PART THREE

MERGING A CONCEPTUAL MAP WITH LEADER BEHAVIORS IN TASK GROUPS

◆ ◆ ◆

Good leadership consists of motivating people to their highest levels by offering them opportunities, not obligations. That is how things happen naturally. Life is an opportunity and not an obligation.

◆

art 3 brings this book to closure. In Chapters 5 and 6, we present some issues for you to grapple with as you plan how to lead and participate in task groups. By reflecting on the model for task groups and making direct connections to leader and member behavior, you will be able to decide what aspects of this model fit your particular group. This section will help you make a direct link between information in this book and the types of groups you work with on a daily basis.

◆

CHAPTER FIVE

Reflections on Task Groups: Changing Paradigms

D uring World War II the U.S. air force flew bombing mission after bombing mission over Germany. Every day the American bomber groups faced death. The German artillery threw everything it had at the planes overhead, frequently devastating both planes and crew members. Under such stressful conditions, bomber crews often became overwhelmed, and many broke down emotionally and psychologically. Nevertheless, others seemed to override the stress and carry on. The high command considered the difference between the crews that fell apart and those that remained intact. Flight leaders were the only differentiating factor. Crews that eventually could not manage the daily missions had leaders who flew "by the book" and took no time to learn about their crew members or to build a spirit of cohesion. In contrast, the flight crews that managed to complete continuous bombing missions without relief were led by officers who showed interest in and concern for their crews yet also managed to fly successfully.

More recently, during the National Basketball Association's playoffs, the New York Knicks set a precedent. The team was the first ever seeded in eighth place to reach the championship finals after overcoming all odds. What was the difference between this team and the highly touted teams it beat on the way to the finals? The clear difference was the coach. Story after story reveals the respect he drew from his players. They explained that their success was due to the care and regard that he showed them as he planned for each game.

These anecdotes tell us that leaders need to balance content and process, as we have underscored in the first four chapters of this book. The anecdotes also dispel the belief that task group members do not wish to be involved with "touchy-feely stuff." However one chooses to define success, teams that succeed have leaders who pay attention to the person-hood of their team members and find ways for members to work coopera-tively and collaboratively. Whether in a successful military operation or a successful basketball season, a leader's attention to process is as important as attention to content in achieving the goals of the group. In other words, process drives content. Process is the steam in the content engine; the value of one depends on the value of the other. Steam spewing forth unbridled by an engine has no value, nor does an engine without the steam necessary to turn it.

Why Have Groups at All?

Why do we bother to bring people together in groups to accomplish tasks in the first place? The simple answer is found in the adage "Two heads are better than one." Thus, it is possible to conclude that whenever two or more people come together to accomplish a task, it should be accom-plished more effectively because it taps into the power of the collective. For example, consider an old-fashioned barn raising, when neighbors gather to erect a barn. Certainly, the work force of the collective is released and is much more effective than it would be if an individual worked to raise the barn alone.

Nevertheless, whenever we bring people together to accomplish a task, the people part often gets overlooked and only the task receives focus. Even in a barn raising, the task is only part of the reason for gather-ing. Visualize how people reach out to one another, talking and asking questions, while food is prepared to feed them all. Visualize collaboration among the workers, including attention to building plans and shared lead-ership functions. In brief, a barn raising balances process and content. It also shows evidence of the four leadership skills mentioned in Chapter 1: caring, meaning attribution, emotional stimulation, and executive func-tion. Moreover, the questions "Who am I?" "Who am I with you?" and "Who are we together?" are addressed in the time it takes to raise the barn from start to finish. Throughout the project we see collaboration among all participants. It is clear, after we have read the first four chapters of this book, why a barn can be raised in a day. Although the barn raisers may not intentionally think of the warm-up, action, and closure phases, evi-dence shows that each phase has occurred. Attention is given to planning the event, resources are in place, collaboration exists, tasks are distributed according to skill and ability, attention is given to the personhood of each group member, food is prepared, and there is celebration at the end for having achieved the group's task.

We have learned from our contributors' stories that everyday task groups do not all mirror the examples of successful flight crew leaders, basketball coaches, or organizers of barn-raising groups. Mary Cathcart tells us, for instance, that her legislative group members would get up and leave if warm-up time were spent on activities that help them get better acquainted. Her group gives little attention to "Who am I?" "Who am I with you?" and "Who are we together?" Her colleagues would just as soon get to "raising the barn" rather than spend time on such process questions. It is easy to see, then, why it takes so long for political groups to get things done! Much blame can be placed on bureaucracy and custom, which encourage task groups to plow through content with little or no attention to process.

In contrast, Alice Cryer-Sumler, Issy Cross, Mary Frenning, Courtland Lee, Al Alcazar, Larry Stokes, Don Reichard, and John Phillips all agree that, while preplanning and clear purpose are important, it is equally as important to help members get to know one another. Personal relationships are a prerequisite for groups to operate effectively. These leaders acknowledge group members as resources and thus position the leader as a person whose task is to release the power of the group in an organized and focused way that will lead to goal attainment.

As we have noted, members of all groups, including task groups, bring to the group their own diverse skills, experiences, background, and culture. In such diversity the power and strength of the task group resides. Yet each of our six fictional leaders—Paul, Reverend Ellison, Letitia, Richard, Jane, and Maria—has avoided, ignored, or minimized such diversity. Lack of attention to diversity can hinder the effectiveness of the task group. Group leaders need to view diversity not as a threat but as a potential asset. They must embrace it and challenge themselves to harness its power. Courtland Lee, Al Alcazar, Don Reichard, Larry Stokes, Alice Cryer-Sumler, Issy Cross, Mary Frenning, and John Phillips encourage coalition building, collaboration, and the development of a group culture as a means for harnessing the energy of the group.

Finally, and very importantly, groups cannot function effectively without clear goals and purposes. Goals are like the rudder of a ship. They help give the group direction and stay its course. Without clear goals and purposes, the group will flounder, become directionless, and eventually cease to function. Therefore, it is imperative that the reasons for forming a group be clear from the outset. Members will then understand their mission. All of our consulting leaders agree that establishing clear goals in the warm-up phase is necessary.

The Challenges of the Action Phase

With the challenge of forming the task group behind them, leaders may breathe a sigh of relief, believing they have met their toughest challenge. Nothing could be further from the truth. The action phase may pose the greatest challenge of all. In the warm-up phase leaders generally maintain a high profile. However, in the action phase they need to maintain lower visibility (i.e., not be a central presence) and allow group members to assume more responsibility and work. A leader's primary concern is to help the group feel empowered to accomplish its task. Of course, accomplishment can only occur if the group has completely evolved through the warm-up phase. Group guidelines must be established, the group's task must be clearly delineated, the three process questions must be addressed, coalitions must begin, collaboration must be encouraged, a structure must be in place to facilitate the achievement of goals, and individual members' strengths must be identified and encouraged. Only then is the task group in a position to assume self-direction. At this point leaders need to demonstrate a range of skills, including process observation, conflict resolution, confrontation, feedback, group norm maintenance, and attention to the here-and-now. Engaging in all of these activities while maintaining a low profile is quite a feat for leaders. Yet as we have learned, our contributors all agree that leaders must attend to these dimensions of leadership.

How often have we heard coaches say, "It is up to the players now. We have done everything we can to prepare them." In effect, coaches are saying that they did all they could during the warm-up phase; the responsibility for taking the team to victory now rests with the players individually and collectively. For those of us who have led a team, the feelings such words conjure up may be familiar. We recall moments when we wanted to enter the fray, believing we could show how a player or the team might benefit from our input. Yet we knew that, as leaders, playing was not our role. We hoped we had prepared the players to assume such responsibility, while we assumed a less active, less leader-centered profile. Coaches on the sidelines continue to engage in leadership activities. Players receive feedback on their play. Sometimes coaches confront players or the team about the manner of play. They exhort their team members and offer observations on how they are playing (i.e., process observations). Coaches keep players focused on the here-and-now, urging them to forget a past error and move on. They help players and the team keep their composure by sticking to the pregame plan (i.e., maintenance of structure) and managing any conflict that arises. All of these leadership activities occur while the players are centrally involved in the drama on the field. It is a challenge for coaches not to become leader-centered and thus create a dependency on the coach. They need to resist such temptation. They need to trust that by engaging in leader behaviors they will release the power of the group. By empowering members and the group, coaches will accomplish their primary task for the action phase.

Clearly, most of our fictional leaders have not begun to position themselves to achieve such an objective. In fact, if they continue on their paths, their groups will probably be leader-centered, and the power within the collective will not be released. Fortunately for our contributors, the converse is true. One by one, they have let us know how they strive to maintain a low profile and allow members to assume leadership responsibilities. Their reflections indicate that they engage in virtually all of the leadership behaviors we have presented to release the power of the collective.

The Importance of Closure

How we end task groups is no less important than how we begin them. Although it is often neglected, the closure phase plays a significant role in the life of the task group. Imagine reading a good book only to discover there is no concluding chapter. Or imagine going to a play where the actors do not appear for the final act. What feelings would you have: a sense of incompleteness, frustration, anger? The same goes for a task group. Members and leaders alike deserve to feel a sense of completion, a time to recognize accomplishments and consider how individual members contributed to the group's goal achievement. The leader deserves feedback on the facilitative or nonfacilitative quality of the behaviors that led the group to the achievement of its goals. Such self-knowledge is important and helps guide future membership and leadership.

As we have noted, the closure phase needs to be seen as an integral part of the group's structure. Our contributors recognize that fact. Our fictional leaders, on the other hand, may see that something needs to happen to close their groups, but they do not understand the power of effective closure or how to implement it. Yet without effective closure, members and leaders may not understand what has happened or how to proceed in the future.

Summary

The concepts of warm-up, action, and closure and the balance between process and content will challenge task group leaders today and in the future. We ask leaders to recognize that process and relationships are central to their conceptual map for task group leadership. It is time to replace the predictable and common model of task groups (which emphasizes content) with a carefully constructed and intentional plan for balancing content with process.

We believe that people can gain much through face-to-face interactions to solve problems and achieve goals. The question facing leaders and members is "Will these face-to-face groups continue following the familiar yet often unproductive path in which process issues are ignored or minimized?" An alternative paradigm is to embrace the role of process and shift the focus from a product-oriented view to one characterized by balance, one that embraces the importance of relationships. While the content-driven model may achieve desired products and outcomes, many members of such groups feel unrecognized, unsatisfied, undervalued, and underused. We must begin to construct ways of interacting and behaving that truly respect the collective energy and contributions of our members. Otherwise, why bring people together in the first place?

After reflecting on the concepts, stories, and insights presented in this book, we find that one particular shift seems to be pivotal. Leaders must move away from the fear, dislike, or discomfort of process activities in task groups to the view that attention to process can facilitate the kind of coalition building that is essential for task groups to be effective and satisfying. This shift will require leaders to become skilled at linking process to content and will challenge them to educate their members to the valuable role that attention to process can play in task groups. Group members who can work together across a diversity of perspectives while engaging in cooperative, collaborative, and respectful exchanges will strengthen the outcomes of any task group.

◆ ◆ ◆

Points to Ponder

1. Explain what "process drives content" means and its significance for task group leaders.

2. Discuss the advantages of a member-centered task group over
a leader-centered task group.

3. List reasons why a focus on content is so attractive in task
groups.

4. List reasons why a focus on process is so difficult in task
groups.

5. As you think about yourself leading a task group, consider the
personal concerns you may have about attending to process.

◆ ◆ ◆

References

Heider, J. (1997). *The tao of leadership.* Atlanta: Humanics New Age.

◆

CHAPTER SIX

Revisiting Our Scenarios: Designs for Implementing Warm-Up, Action, and Closure in Task Groups

Throughout this book you have read about the importance of reflection, meaning attribution, and the value of taking time to recognize accomplishments, both in terms of content outcomes in task groups and the way in which process contributes to those outcomes. You have been asked to consider ways to build attention to closure in your task groups and to honor the work of all group members. The importance of closure has been emphasized repeatedly. Now, as we prepare to close this book and as we have asked you to do in your groups, we summarize, discuss our favorite learning points, and present six task group designs that can serve as maps for your future work as task group leaders.

Our model for task group practice embraces two important points. First, groups work best when there is a balance between process and content. Second, balance is best achieved through attention to warm-up, action, and closure. Leaders who keep these points in mind as they design and conduct task groups will maximize the chances that their groups will be successful and satisfying. One of the primary learning points for leaders to remember is that all activities designed to facilitate coalition building and interactions must be strategically and clearly linked to why the task group has been formed in the first place. Without that connection among "Who am I?" "Who am I with you?" and "What do we have to do?" there is a danger of losing the power and credibility of the desired group outcome. Our contributors have highlighted these concepts in their rich stories and descriptions.

We now pull from our model for task groups some suggestions in the form of a group design for each of our six fictional leaders. As you read the designs, think back to earlier chapters, especially to the illustrations of the model in our contributors' stories.

Paul's Landscaping Business Group

◆

Paul started a landscaping business several years ago. Because of increased demand, he has hired six new staff members who have lots of ideas and energy. Paul plans to bring all of them together so they can meet one another and develop a sense of teamwork. He wants to harness their energy and excitement while making sure that everyone works for the good of the business. Some members seem open to the idea of group meetings, while others just want to do their job and avoid what they perceive as "touchy-feely" time. Paul is determined to host this group in a few weeks and wonders how to make his team-building effort useful and satisfying for everyone.

The Conceptual Picture

One thing operating in Paul's favor is the fact that he is thinking ahead about this group meeting. In the planning phase he has the opportunity to prepare a beginning that will launch his group idea in a positive direction. Throughout the book, we have emphasized the importance of planning, preparing, and thinking strategically about what is possible. Here Paul needs a plan, a blueprint to guide his behavior.

What does Paul know? He knows that some of his staff responded well to his initial presentation of this group idea. He knows that others are not particularly open to what they see as touchy-feely and a waste of time. Therefore, Paul needs to take both responses into consideration as he designs his critical first meeting. The goal of team building naturally brings a focus on process—on the relationships among members. Paul wants to create a successful climate and attend to these process issues while keeping in mind the reason for doing so: to strengthen and expand his business. As we have noted earlier, leaders need to attend to some type of people orientation, while being tuned to the link between this orientation and the purpose of the group.

Paul recognizes the strengths and resources that each of his employees brings to his business. They may not know much about each other's strengths and resources; therefore, he will want to plan some activities that fit his population and setting and will help him reach his goal of cooperation and collaboration among his staff.

Suggested Design for Paul's First Meeting

As a first step, Paul can prepare an agenda in which he states the purpose of this meeting, the location, timelines, and his hopes about what will happen. This agenda can be handed out to his staff before the meeting and thereby function as an advanced organizer for the upcoming meeting (Hulse-Killacky & Killacky, 1997). The literature on group work reinforces the view that structure provided early on in a group can actually decrease member anxiety and increase the likelihood that members will openly share their feelings and thoughts (Bednar, Melnick, & Kaul, 1974). With a clear purpose, an agenda in hand, and Paul's understanding of what he wants to see happen in the group, he will be able to create an atmosphere that is likely to dispel the negative concerns of a few of his employees.

Next, Paul needs to select a meeting space that will be comfortable for seven people. Offering refreshments sets an inviting tone and allows people to mingle and get acquainted before the meeting starts. It is important for Paul to be as relaxed as possible. Being relaxed and centered helps leaders in all types of situations pay attention to what is actually occurring and to use here-and-now observations to serve the group endeavor (Heider, 1997). Paul already knows that several members of his staff are receptive; he needs to create a welcoming atmosphere that conveys his optimism that this meeting can be a satisfying and useful experience for all members.

Once everyone arrives and has a chance to informally interact, Paul can begin the meeting. Arranging the furniture so that everyone can see everyone else is helpful. Paul can determine the arrangement based on what he knows about his staff. The agenda can be used as a starting place for the meeting. He might want to reiterate his desire for staff to get better acquainted and to learn about each other's strengths and resources so that as a group they can brainstorm and implement better and richer ideas for keeping this business successful and thriving.

An opening round could involve asking staff members to give their name, what they particularly enjoy about landscaping work, and what special skills or abilities they bring to this job. One of the keys to Paul's success with this first meeting will be his ability to make links between the information gained in the opening round and the purpose of the group. By doing so, he will balance process and content and provide meaningful experiences for his staff.

Warm-up for Paul will include mingling, his opening comments, and the opening round. As members become acquainted around similarities and differences, he can shift to the action phase, indicating that he wants to brainstorm some ideas for strengthening the business. During this phase, Paul will want to pay attention to who talks and who needs drawing out. His attention to process will help create a group culture in which all voices can be heard. Through conversations he might discover that certain staff members have special talents and ideas that blend well with the talents and ideas of others. By reflecting on the variety of talents and skills, Paul can reinforce the possibilities for cooperation and collaboration that fit his team-building theme. He may also want to use the group to prioritize any suggestions that have surfaced and determine who is going to tackle what activity or job.

As the meeting winds down, Paul will want to focus on the closure phase. What was it like to get together and discuss each person's different ideas, skills, and perspectives? What was it like to get to know each other a little more? Paul can thank his staff for participating and ask whether they want to get together again. If future meetings are desired, Paul will need to discuss with his staff the details about the next meeting and who will be responsible for certain tasks. He will want to give members an opportunity to express feelings about how the meeting worked or did not work and what they will take from this meeting to apply to their landscaping roles. Providing some reflection time to address these questions and to evaluate the success of the meeting will help all participants move from this session to their work outside the group, which fits with Paul's original goal for the session.

Reverend Ellison's Church Group

◆

The Reverend Ellison has called together local church members for their first fall meeting, scheduled for 7:00–8:30 P.M. Some members arrive on time, others late; so he begins about 7:15. He has an agenda, but conversation centers on other issues. Several members tell the new music minister all about church politics; another, who chairs the education committee, critiques a new restaurant in town. The structured part of the meeting finally gets underway with a few reports mingled with interruptions, especially from several vocal members of the council. As 8:30 approaches, only a few items on the agenda have been addressed. Several members observe, "I thought this meeting was over at 8:30. I have other things to do." There is much shifting in chairs as people check the clock and pack up their materials. Reverend Ellison has not addressed the pacing and timing of the evening session and has not checked with members to see if it is okay to extend the meeting time.

The Conceptual Picture

Unlike Paul, Reverend Ellison is in charge of a group that has met before and meets on a regular basis throughout the year. Already there should be group norms in place that clarify the purpose of the group and indicate the established guidelines for starting and ending times. It is not clear from his scenario, however, that such norms have been developed. To his credit, Reverend Ellison does have an agenda, and we can assume that all members have received an advance copy. Reverend Ellison's plan for the evening is to smoothly execute this agenda, cover a certain amount of church business, and adjourn in a timely manner. However, there are some blocks to attaining his goals.

One block has to do with expectations. It seems likely that church members may have expectations that differ from Reverend Ellison's. While there seems to be a general desire to finish up at 8:30, the definition of content (i.e., "What is our point for being here?") appears to vary. Members have multiple and competing agendas. In addition, the meeting involves both returning members and new members; therefore, all members may not be acquainted with everyone in the room. In this situation, what is Reverend Ellison to do?

Suggested Design for Reverend Ellison's Church Meeting

When people convene in a new cycle of task group meetings, there is always some degree of turnover. That is what has happened in Reverend Ellison's church group. He needs to design a warm-up activity that taps the energy of those present and addresses the changes in composition. The questions "Who am I?" and "Who am I with you?" seem most appropriate to consider. In church settings, one might think that everyone knows everyone else. That assumption is sometimes faulty. During an opening round, members could give their name and function on the committee. New members could be welcomed and all participants reminded of each person's role. Reverend Ellison can observe that knowing names and committee roles will help everyone grasp the many tasks and duties that contribute to successfully running the church.

At this point it is important for Reverend Ellison to take an active stance and give an overview of the purpose of the meeting. The agenda and group norms could be posted on newsprint for everyone to see. If there are no formal group norms, then he could propose some in the form of a list, ask for any additions, and address any questions. Recall Don Reichard's list of ground rules for his community-based programming coalition group (Chapter 2). His list attended to both the process (i.e., how business was to be conducted) and content (i.e., the purpose, goals, and actions of members). As in Don's group, Reverend Ellison could invite feedback by asking if members understand and support the ground rules. The value of ground rules cannot be overemphasized. They provide direction for both content and process. Posted ground rules can be referred to when things seem off task or when members are not listening to or respecting others. Reverend Ellison might say to his church group members, "I know that many of you are busy and have other obligations after this meeting ends. I want us to use our time well. So you may see me stopping the action from time to time, making sure that we are on target with our agenda and ensuring that everyone has a chance to speak on various issues. I will leave ample time before 8:30 to review our work and to make sure that you all know what your responsibilities are between now and our next meeting." This clarifies that he is going to be watching the process and paying attention to the content as well.

As the meeting moves into the action phase, which includes hearing various committee reports, Reverend Ellison now has a structure in place to cut off extraneous conversations when needed and to hold or shift the focus to make sure that certain items get attention. Often agendas have more content than is possible to consider in a 90-minute meeting. If it becomes clear that there is too much on the agenda to adequately accomplish in the given time frame, Reverend Ellison will want to prioritize items with the help of the group and decide which are most urgent for this particular meeting. Perhaps there are tasks that others can work on in smaller subgroups. Members can discuss and agree on such contingency plans.

Throughout the meeting, especially near the end, Reverend Ellison will want to summarize what has taken place and note the remaining time so that members have a sense of how the evening is progressing. Pacing and sequencing are leader skills that help meetings flow. Providing brief summaries gives meaning to the events in the meeting and keeps track of the big picture. Near 8:15 Reverend Ellison will want to stop the action and assess the situation. Will all items be covered? If not, who will do what between now and the next meeting to gather information, carry out a project, or bring material to the next meeting? He can also check in with members in the form of a closing round to assess how the meeting has worked for them and what suggestions they may have for future meetings. As in all group situations, he will want to close by offering his appreciation for everyone's presence and their contributions to the evening's meeting. His behavior as a leader is purposeful and reflects a deliberate move. By behaving as described, he intentionally focuses on norm building and the development of a culture that is characterized by collaboration and cooperation. These are exactly the qualities that he wants to reinforce.

Letitia's Legislative Education Subcommittee

Letitia has just been appointed to the education subcommittee of the state legislature. This subcommittee is comprised of members of both major political parties. Although it is early in the legislative session and the subcommittee has only met a few times, she has been happy with how members have addressed various tasks and at the friendly nature of the exchanges during their deliberations. At this particular meeting members are charged with making budget decisions, but for some reason other topics have taken priority. Just as Letitia realizes that there are only 15 minutes left in the meeting, several restless members start looking at their watches. One states, "I've got to go now; I forgot to tell you that I have another meeting across the street." Another jumps up: "Oh, I have to meet Representative Smith in a few minutes. . . . Gotta run." Letitia feels a sense of dread. The task is not complete, and these members are leaving without discussing how they plan to help make these looming budget decisions.

The Conceptual Picture

Letitia's group reminds us of Reverend Ellison's group in that there appears to be some confusion about content focus as well as a need for active leader direction regarding the pacing and sequencing of the meeting. In addition, Letitia faces a common problem in task groups composed of members who have other things to do: they often just get up and leave. In her favor is the members' friendly demeanor, a good quality in a group of people who have differing political viewpoints. Since this group is still in the formative stage, having only met a few times, Letitia has the opportunity to work with her members to establish some ground rules for attendance and participation. It is impractical to believe that members of a legislative group will not have multiple interruptions that may cause them to leave early or arrive late. As we noted in a previous chapter, all task groups are characterized by members who have busy lives and competing schedules. Given the legislators' situations, Letitia can still provide a structure for dialogue about how to address these disruptions. After all, the point of the subcommittee is to address education issues, and this content requires primary attention. By highlighting the need to develop a procedure for meeting the task while being sensitive to everyone's sched-ule, she will address both content and process issues. Perhaps the meeting time could be changed; there may be other logistical interventions that might prove helpful here. In addition, after some ground rules are in place, Letitia will be able to refer back to those ground rules to support her efforts to pace and sequence during the meeting.

Using reflection and pauses will also help Letitia. She needs a mecha-nism in place that is understood and supported by her members so she can check in periodically to assess how the meeting is progressing. And she could benefit from the use of check-in rounds, which may help her learn what kinds of expectations and restraints on time are present in a particular meeting. In short, Letitia should be hopeful because her group is relatively new and thus has the potential to be flexible. She can use a variety of leader skills to help change the way these meetings take place.

Suggested Design for Letitia's Legislative Education Subcommittee Meeting

As a first step, Letitia can send out a short memo to her members indicat-ing that she would like to spend time with the group at the beginning of the next meeting to consider some ground rules that will help ensure that they use their time wisely. She can acknowledge their busy schedules and also remind them that the subcommittee was formed to accomplish certain goals. She can ask her members to bring their suggestions for improving the quality of their meetings. She can conclude her memo by stressing the importance of developing a procedure to address members' comings and goings. Finally, she can attach a proposed agenda for the next meeting.

When the next meeting begins, Letitia can remind members that she needs to take a few minutes to work with them to develop some ground rules for attendance and participation so that, when early departures or other disruptions occur, the work of the group will be minimally affected. These ground rules can be posted on newsprint for everyone to see at every meeting. Through this type of warm-up, Letitia and her members can set a tone for how they will proceed during this and future meetings.

Suggested ground rules might be to (1) show up on time or leave a message with one of the members; (2) review the agenda to set priorities based on time allocation and member attendance; (3) be prepared for the meeting, ready to fully participate in all discussions; (4) let the chair know if someone has to leave early; and (5) allow time for summaries and reflec-tion so that everyone is clear about responsibilities between meetings and how to prepare for the next meeting.

Letitia is now ready to move into the action phase and to focus on the content for the day. For example, if budget issues are the topic, she can structure the discussion, paying attention to time, pacing, sequencing and providing occasional summaries to help all participants assess the tempo and goal accomplishments. She will want to practice cutting off, drawing out, and holding and shifting the focus as needed. Periodically she can stop and ask members, "How is the meeting going? Are we doing what we need to be doing?"

Certain members may have to leave early; if so, there is a structure in place now to address those early departures. Letitia and her members can assess the work of the subcommittee and determine what is left to do and who will be responsible for attending to various tasks. After a member leaves, Letitia can return to the agenda and tackle other items, knowing that the departing member is clear about his duties. As the meeting moves into the closure phase, Letitia can offer a few summaries of the meeting's accomplishments and work with members to finalize what each person's next steps will be. After the meeting, Letitia should remember to keep a copy of the ground rules so that she can post them at future meetings.

Jane's Local Professional Organization Meeting

◆

Jane is the new president of a local professional organization with a membership encompassing different races, ethnicities, ages, sexual orientations, and genders. She is presiding over a monthly board meeting in which budget issues are being discussed. This topic sets off strong disagreements. When an older lesbian board member expresses her viewpoint about making sure money is allocated to support the needs of gay and lesbian youth in the area, several members start screaming at her. She continues to push her point, while others loudly express their different convictions. Jane becomes overwhelmed and cannot create order. She adjourns the meeting.

The Conceptual Picture

Here is a collection of well-meaning people who have a passion for certain issues and who need a mechanism to voice their own needs and to listen, understand, and respect the positions of others. Budget discussions can be heated because in many community organizations money is scarce. As a result, group members may really pursue their particular pet projects. The diversity in Jane's group could be a positive force (i.e., many viewpoints, resources, strengths, perspectives). It seems that these diverse viewpoints are being underused and are the source of attacks and rancorous exchanges. No wonder Jane is overwhelmed.

What seems to be missing is any indication that members have had an orientation to each other—time to build a culture of cooperation, collaboration, and mutual respect. Conyne (1989) asks task group leaders to balance attention between orientation to purpose and orientation to people. In Jane's group, however, time for culture building has been almost nonexistent. Task group members need safety, just as members in other types of groups do. But this group does not seem to have a climate of safety and respect, meaning that Jane has some challenges ahead. Taking time for people to learn about their differences can clear up misconceptions and create a climate in which alliances can be developed to address the group's goals. Jane's group needs ground rules—some type of structure that helps all participants understand how the group's business will be conducted.

Suggested Design for Jane's Professional Organization Meeting

Let's start by attending to the immediate crisis in Jane's group. If the explosion happened early in the life of the organization's meetings, Jane will have a better chance of success than if these behaviors have been building up for some time. At the beginning of the next meeting, she can state up front that she is concerned about the display of rancor that occurred at the last meeting. She needs to invite and engage her members to backtrack—to reexamine issues that should have been addressed in the first meeting. Taking an optimistic stance, she can ask members to write down (1) their expectations for being on this board, (2) their expectations of their colleagues, (3) their expectations of Jane, and (4) what they need to see happen to make these board meetings satisfying and successful. After writing down their responses, Jane can invite discussion and begin to draw some themes from the various statements. This discussion can lead to a consensus statement on attendance and participation that can be posted for everyone to see and review in this meeting and future ones.

Moving into the action phase, Jane may want to consider a movement activity in which she asks members to move around the room based on certain demographic and descriptive information. Here are some possible topics:

- Country of origin
- Length of time in the community
- Learning style preferences: talk things out, think things through, have the specifics, or see the big picture
- Comfort with giving and receiving feedback
- Marital and family status: parents or not; single or partnered
- Special needs
- Cultural identification
- Liberal or conservative positions on economic or social issues

Such activities show where people are similar and different in relation to a range of issues that might be important for this group to know. Jane can help by pointing out where certain perspectives, resources, and strengths can combine with other perspectives, resources, and strengths to work for the good of the organization's goals. This is a heavy task. Jane needs to let her members know that she recognizes that these discussions may be hard but explain why they are critically important if this group is to move ahead in a healthy direction.

The goal of these various culture-building activities is not only to clarify the purpose for group members but to create a climate that can enhance rather than hinder the work of the group. Jane needs to take time as she proceeds through these activities to reflect on what is happening, what is being learned, and how participating in these activities is influencing relationships in the group.

As the meeting ends, Jane can ask her members to comment in a closing round about their experiences in the meeting. What have they learned about themselves, about others? How will they use the information learned in this meeting in future meetings as they grapple with difficult decisions? As we have noted, leaders must help members of task groups recognize the link between activities that are geared toward process issues and the purpose of the group. Such a link strengthens the possibility that members will appreciate the role of relationships in attaining task goals.

Jane's scenario reminds us that task leaders need to spend time developing a strong warm-up phase. In the design we have just presented, Jane is trying to catch up after having experienced an unpleasant event. Leaders must expect unpleasant things to happen in task groups. However, when they plan carefully and attend to the assumptions that underlie the model for task groups presented in this book, they will minimize the likelihood of such events. But if challenging and disruptive moments do occur, leaders will have a structure in place to quickly address them.

Richard's English Department Teachers' Meeting

◆

Richard is the chair of the English department at a large high school. At the beginning of the school year he calls a teachers' meeting to discuss how to implement a state-mandated English program. By the end of the first 20 minutes, it becomes apparent that three first-year teachers who have recently graduated from well-respected teacher education programs are intent on presenting their ideas from current research literature. Older teachers, unhappy with their new colleagues, find these ideas unrealistic. One responds, "I remember we tried a similar idea 16 years ago, and it didn't work." This teacher then begins a detailed story about the history of the high school's English program. Richard looks around the room at signs of verbal and nonverbal dissatisfaction. He knows that if the different viewpoints and perspectives are not quickly addressed and integrated, the teaching team will be ineffective or fall apart.

The Conceptual Picture

Like Paul, Reverend Ellison, and Letitia, Richard has the advantage of being at the front end of a task group effort and will be able to intervene and address developing problems. It seems that he has not warmed up his group members in a way that might make it easier for two different subsets of people to engage cooperatively and collaboratively. It also seems likely that the newer teachers are developing certain impressions of the veteran teachers while the veteran teachers are developing opinions about the newer teachers; in both cases, these impressions may be misconstrued and inaccurate. Without some effort to bridge this growing gap, these opinions will certainly impede Richard's attempt to build a working group.

Once again we must consider the warm-up phase, including systematic planning and thoughtful preparation. It is not clear if Richard previously realized that this polarity existed in his group; if he did, he did not act immediately on that knowledge. Right away we can speculate that insecurity, safety, and power are at issue. The leader needs to devise some way to help these potentially competing subsets of members get to know one another and start building a culture that is characterized by cooperation, collaboration, and mutual respect.

In addition, the leader must develop both content and process questions regarding achievement of the task at hand: implementing a state-mandated English program. How many meetings will be needed to address this task? What are the state's expectations for when the final plan is to be completed? Balanced with these content questions should be ones that ask members to articulate their expectations for being in these meetings and being with each other. Using the answers to these questions, Richard can design meetings in which members are oriented to the group's purpose and to one other.

Suggested Design for Richard's Teachers' Meeting

For the warm-up phase of this meeting, Richard can begin with several statements to the group as a whole. First, he can convey his recognition of the different and important resources and strengths that each member brings. Second, he can acknowledge that the task ahead will require the participation and talents of the entire collective. Third, he can express his hope that these various skills, experiences, and talents can be used cooperatively and collaboratively to address the task before the faculty. What Richard is doing in these opening statements is setting a tone; he is letting the group know that he recognizes the unique gifts that each brings to this enterprise. He is also establishing a cultural norm as well as making known his agenda (expectations) for the group.

As warm-up continues, Richard needs to ensure that members embrace his viewpoint. He can strengthen that possibility by giving them a chance to get acquainted, to build connections and break down any walls based on initial impressions. An opening round is one option. He can ask members to introduce themselves, talk about what excites them about teaching English, and what their hopes and plans are for the new school year. As they talk, Richard can look for ways to link them around similarities and point out differences as examples of special skills and abilities that certain members bring. For example, the historical perspective given by one of the veteran teachers could be instructive and helpful to the group as they begin to discuss ways to implement the state-mandated program. Rather than getting irritated or angry with this teacher, Richard, using a range of skills, can help the newer teachers see her as a potential resource. Likewise, as newer teachers talk about their excitement about current research that they bring from their training programs, Richard can make connections between new information and the group's goal.

As we noted in previous designs, the development of ground rules is important to the healthy functioning of a task group. Deciding on norms for attendance and participation can build a structure that Richard can return to when discussions get off track or seem unproductive. Simply asking members, "What would make our meetings most enjoyable and useful for you?" can begin a dialogue that demonstrates the leader's attention to both process and content and reinforces the norms of collaboration and cooperation. As the action phase of the meeting continues, Richard can reiterate the need for active listening and mutual respect. By paying attention to the here-and-now, Richard can uncover potential problems before they become too big. For example, if members roll their eyes or sigh as discussion shifts to the implementation plans, Richard might check with the group to see if the conversation is on track. Skills of cutting off, drawing out, and holding and shifting the focus will be helpful to him in this meeting. They keep a focus on content and are useful when the leader wants to attend to process issues.

As the closure phase of the meeting approaches, Richard should thank members for their contributions and for their willingness to help develop a structure for this meeting and upcoming ones. By doing so, he again offers supportive feedback about members' efforts to collaborate and cooperate. He should summarize their content accomplishments and make sure that members understand what their particular tasks are before the next meeting, thereby assuring no misunderstandings or ambiguity about responsibilities. A closing round could be used to give each teacher a chance to give Richard some feedback on the meeting and to offer any suggestions to help strengthen future ones. This procedure helps members take ownership of the process and content of their meetings.

Maria's Community Recreation Committee

◆

Maria has been asked by the town council to facilitate several meetings for the local community recreation committee. The purpose of this evening's meeting is to begin discussions about a location for the new community playground. Maria knows who the committee members are and recognizes that some people are opinionated and like to talk, while others are quieter and more reflective. She wants to make sure that members stay on task and that everyone's ideas are included. She wonders if she can help create a setting in which all members can contribute to the task in meaningful ways.

The Conceptual Picture

First, it is important to recognize that, unlike some of the other groups we have discussed, Maria's group is time-limited. The committee will have two to three sessions to make a site selection for the children's playground. Often in community-based committees, representatives come from a variety of work settings, and people differ in terms of social and economic status. Maria is already aware that, along with excitement about this project, there may be different levels of verbal and work styles; and she wants everyone to be actively involved in discussions.

Maria's job is to accelerate the process of establishing a working climate because she knows that there will only be a few meetings. Her desire to balance process and content requires careful planning and preparation. What can she do to involve everyone and keep an eye on the reason for having these meetings in the first place?

Suggested Design for Maria's Community Recreation Committee Meeting

Maria will find the questions "Who am I?" "Who am I with you?" and "What do we have to do?" very helpful to consider as she begins her first meeting. Like Richard, she may want to begin with a welcoming statement that communicates her recognition of the many and varied strengths and resources represented on this committee. She can mention her hope that everyone will contribute to these conversations, which will have a great impact on reaching the goal of a long-awaited playground. Noting that there is limited time available to tackle this project, she can explain that she wants to create a climate where everyone can feel safe and comfortable about offering ideas and suggestions. Then she can lead an opening round in which members introduce themselves and state their reasons for being on the committee. At the end of the round, she can observe that the high level of excitement about this project may easily lead to multiple conversations. Maria can propose a few ground rules to guide discussion and the decision-making process. For example, one person speaks at a time, everyone who wishes to speak gets a turn, and all ideas are welcome. Ground rules can be approved and posted for everyone to see.

To facilitate the action phase, which will be focused on brainstorming ideas for playground sites, she can check out several style preferences. For example, she can ask, "Who likes to speak up first? Who likes to ponder and think things through? Who likes to get the job done quickly? Who likes to keep options open for further discussion?" Answers to these questions can give her information to use as she observes how members interact. Back to the group task, she can now hand out paper to group members and ask them to complete the sentence "My wish for a recreation playground location is. . . . " By using the ground rules and the information from the style preferences discussion, she can facilitate a brainstorming session. Potential locations can be posted on newsprint, and then members can select several top sites to explore. Subsets of members can be formed to gather information about a particular site regarding availability, price, advantages, and so on, which can be disseminated at the next meeting. To encourage heterogeneity, Maria can pair up members from diverse backgrounds. For example, the janitor from the local high school can be paired with the president of a local business; a faculty member at the university can be paired with a clerk in the local supermarket.

As closure approaches, Maria will want to make sure that all members are aware of their various responsibilities and what information will be needed at the next meeting. She can initiate a closing round to evaluate what worked and what did not. Members can state their reactions to the meeting and the conversations. In this way Maria conveys her desire to have members feel invested in the group and show that she sees collaboration and cooperation as occurring through all phases of the group.

Summary

All of our fictional leaders now have some direction for their task groups. In each design, process and content issues were balanced through attention to warm-up, action, and closure. As you consider your own task group settings, you can use this set of questions to guide your preparation for leadership (adapted from Hulse-Killacky & Killacky, 1997):

1. Do I have a plan for what I think is possible to strive for in this task group? In other words, if this group is successful, what kinds of things need to happen?

2. Do I have some information about the participants attending this group?

3. Knowing what I know about the participants in this group and the purpose of the group, what can I do to help develop effective communication among participants?

4. Before the group meeting, would it be helpful for participants to receive planning materials and an overview of the first meeting?

5. At the first meeting, what are some ways to help participants address their expectations about being members of the group, their expectations of other participants, and their expectations of the leader?

6. How will guidelines be developed for how the group goes about its job? By consensus? In written form?

7. How can the meeting time be used so that all members of the group have an opportunity to help set the agenda?

8. How can I (as member or leader) check in from time to time to see if the needs of the group members are being met?

9. What are my plans to help all participants express differences, give and receive feedback, and address conflict when it occurs?

10. Do I feel comfortable and confident about using the skills of cutting off, drawing out, and holding and shifting the focus?

11. What can I do to make sure that there is time for a warm-up activity and time for a closing round at each meeting?

12. What can I do to (a) help participants reflect and make meaning of the work they are doing in the task group and (b) plan for future group activities?

You now have a conceptual framework to guide your work in task groups. Please write us and tell us how the ideas presented in this book contribute to your leadership and membership in task groups. If you have ideas of how to enhance our message in this book, please contact us:

Diana Hulse-Killacky
Department of Educational Leadership, Counseling, and
    Foundations
University of New Orleans
New Orleans, LA 70148
e-mail: dhulseki@uno.edu

We close by returning to John Heider's (1997, p. 53) quotation offered at the beginning of Part 1, which captures the essence of this book's central message:

The wise leader's ability does not rest on techniques or gimmicks or set exercises. The method of awareness-of-process applies to all people and all situations.

◆ ◆ ◆

Points to Ponder

1. Name the parts of these designs that make the most sense to you and your task group setting.

2. Describe the steps you will take to plan and prepare for your task group.

3. Write out a design for your task group that (a) balances process and content issues and (b) ensures that a link will be made between relationship issues and the purpose of the group.

4. As you think about your leadership style in task groups, select one of the following that best represents you at this time: (a) you lean toward a process focus, (b) you lean toward a content focus, (c) you lean toward a focus on both process and content.

5. Describe the strengths and limitations of your selection in point 4. State your plan for building on your strengths and addressing areas for improvement.

6. Several distortions of the model for task groups are illustrated as figures throughout the book. Which of those distortions challenges you most as a task group leader? What ideas do you have for addressing those distortions in your particular group?

7. List your one major learning point after reading this book.

8. List one thing you will do differently in your next task group meeting as a leader or as a member.

9. Every leader's behavior is prompted by some intention. There is a reason or purpose behind what leaders do. Consider the part that leader intentionally will play in your task groups. Consider what you would like to see happen and then figure out ways to bring your intentions to life in your task groups.

◆ ◆ ◆

References

Bednar, R. L., Melnick, J., & Kaul, T. J. (1974). Risk, responsibility and structure: A conceptual framework for initiating group counseling and psychotherapy. *Journal of Counseling Psychology, 21*, 31–37.

Conyne, R. K. (1989). *How personal growth and task groups work.* Newbury Park, CA: Sage.

Heider, J. (1997). *The tao of leadership.* Atlanta: Humanics New Age.

Hulse-Killacky, D., & Killacky, J. (1997). Making coalitions work: Creating a viable environment. *Community College Journal of Research and Practice, 21*(5), 509–517.

Index